Mediterranean Air Fryer Cookbook for Beginners on a Budget

1900 Days of Tasty Recipes that Anyone Can Do in 30 mins or less. Comprehensive Air Fryer Starter Guidebook & 2-Week Meal Plan Included

---

By

Wilda Buckley

TABLE OF CONTENTS

CHAPTER 4: Meal Options 40

CHAPTER 5: Vegetables Recipes 59

CHAPTER 6: Snacks & Appetizers 76

CHAPTER 7: Beans and Grains 94

CHAPTER 8: Pork & Lamb Options..102

CHAPTER 9: Beef Options...108

INTRODUCTION

An air fryer is a kitchenette appliance that heats food by circulating warm air using a convection mechanism. It is a smaller version of the traditional convection oven. A mechanical fan mixes the warm air round the food at great speed, which allows the food to cook and produces a crispier layer due to the browning responses of caramelization and the Maillard reaction. The Maillard reaction requires temperatures of between 140 to 165 °C (284 to 329 °F), while caramelization temperatures require the caramelization of sugar and range from 110 to 180 °C (230 to 356 °F).

Food has always been a passion of many people. You will always enjoy the flavor created when certain ingredients are combined and the various renditions of classic recipes that you can quickly whip up in my kitchen. The only challenge you will experience when it comes to food is not realizing which foods contributed to my well-being and which were not. You would stuff whatever tasted good down my throat without considering the healthier alternatives or exceptions to the dish. Many studies have shown the Mediterranean diet to reduce the risk of cancers, heart disease, diabetes, and levels of bad cholesterol.

The Mediterranean diet food pyramid emphasizes the importance of incorporating leafy vegetables, fruits, legumes, whole grains, and lean protein in my diet while consuming decadent foods like ice-cream or a glass of wine on very few occasions. The Mediterranean diet is more of a lifestyle than a militant diet, which encourages the creation of new eating habits.

In this cookbook, some of the most delicious Mediterranean diet recipes are gathered over the years that are extremely popular among people. However, there is a twist. The recipes are all made using one of the most highly talked-about kitchen gadgets—an air fryer. Get ready to learn how to make innovative meals that promote balanced well-being!

CHAPTER NO. 1
Fundamentals of Mediterranean Air Fryer

If you were under the impression that adopting a Mediterranean way of life would require you to give up fried foods, you need to revise your thinking. Thanks to the widespread dissemination of the air fryer, it is now possible to concoct scrumptious dishes with a Mediterranean flavor that are not saturated in oil and do not threaten one's wellbeing. The reality is that the procedure of deep-frying food adds much more fat to the dish than prepares the food using other ways of cooking. For instance, a battered and deep-fried alternative to oven-roasted chicken breast includes 13.2 grams of fat for every 100 grams, whereas oven-roasted chicken breast comprises only 0.39 grams per 100 grams. Even though this information is available, many individuals would still choose to consume the deep-fried chicken breast rather than the chicken breast that has been oven-roasted since the taste and texture of the former is superior to that of the latter.

Consuming fried food is no longer associated with feelings of guilt thanks to the invention of the air fryer, which employs an entirely new method to produce the same satisfyingly crunchy texture. This makes it possible for those concerned about their health to enjoy fried dishes with less fat than those prepared in a deep fryer. To get the same level of crispiness as deep-fried items, food is circulated in an air fryer as it cooks. The primary difference between air frying and traditional frying is that the former requires just a small percentage of the oil needed for the latter to get the same results in terms of taste and consistency. To put it another way, the air fryer eliminates the use of oils that are heavy in fat and calories from the process of frying dishes. To get crispy chicken, sweet potatoes, or kale chips, all you need is one teaspoon of frying oil instead of the many cups that are often required.

When used appropriately, air fryers can confer several positive health effects on their users. To begin, it may assist in the reduction of excess body fat. Those who often indulge in fried meals will have a lower calorie intake if they prepare their favorite fried dishes using an air fryer rather than a traditional deep fryer. Second, compared to conventional deep fryers, air fryers have a far lower risk of injury during usage. To properly deep fry food, you must first bring a saucepan or pot filled to the brim with oil to a very high temperature. When the oil becomes too hot, there is a good chance that it may spill or spatter over the cooktop, causing burns to anyone who comes into contact with it. Even though air fryers become rather hot, there is no danger of being burnt by the oil inside of them when you use them. Despite this, it is always advisable to follow the instructions in the air fryer handbook to ensure that the cooking process is safe and easy.

In addition, if you cook meals using the conventional way of deep frying, you risk being exposed to harmful substances such as acrylamide, which may occur in some foods due to the process of deep frying. For example, acrylamide has been associated with an increased risk of developing cancer, including ovarian, breast, endometrial, and pancreatic cancer. By making the simple move to using an air fryer, you can significantly lower your exposure to acrylamide and other carcinogenic chemicals produced during cooking at high temperatures.

1.1 Air Fryer and It's Working

The food in an air fryer is cooked by circulation of hot air, as opposed to the traditional method of submerging the food in oil.

The frying chamber of the air fryer draws heat from a heating element that is located adjacent to the food, which results in the food being cooked more quickly.

A fan blows hot air all around the food in the oven.

The temperature is maintained by discharging the surplus hot air that is generated via the exhaust at the rear of the Air Fryer. The aperture, also known as the vent, is located at the top of the Air Fryer.

It is also utilized to combat any increases in the pressure found inside the body.

Depending on the type, the temperatures inside may reach as high as 230 degrees Celsius (445 degrees Fahrenheit).

It is imperative that you do not put oil inside the air fryer and that you do not have combustible items near the air fryer. This is for your own safety.

In compared to conventional ovens, the air fryer typically results in a time savings of around 20% throughout the cooking process.

This varies depending on the kind of air fryer as well as the amount of food that is being prepared in the air fryer.

The Maillard reaction is brought about by traditional techniques of frying, which include totally immersing meals in heated oil, which may reach temperatures far higher than water that is boiling.

The desired meal is coated in a small layer of oil before being placed in the air fryer, which then uses air heated to up to 200 degrees Celsius (392 degrees Fahrenheit) to provide heat and start the reaction.

As a consequence of this, the kitchen equipment is able to brown meals such as fish, French fries, potato chips, cheeseburgers, steak, pastries or poultry while consuming between 70 and 80 percent less oil than a conventional deep fryer.

The temperature and length of time may often be adjusted on modern air fryers, allowing for more exact control over the frying process.

The food is prepared in a cooking basket that is placed above a drip tray while it is being cooked.

To ensure that the food receives an equal coating of oil and cooks in an even manner, the basket has to be shook often.

The more costly fryers do this by combining a food agitator with a mixing mechanism that continually shakes the food as it is being cooked.

However, the majority of air fryers still need the chef to manually complete the process.

Convection ovens and air fryers cook food in a manner that is comparable; however, air fryers are often more compact in both size and volume than convection ovens and produce a lower overall level of heat.

Because a greater quantity of oil is used in traditional frying, it permeates the food (or the coating batter, if one is used) and imparts a flavor that is distinct from that imparted by air frying. As a result, the taste and consistency of foods prepared using traditional frying techniques are not the same as those prepared using air frying techniques.

Because the food in air fryers is covered in a damp batter rather than a dry covering similar breadcrumbs, and because the batter remains firmly on the surface of the food, the fan in the air fryer is able to blow the batter off the food, which ensures that the food cooks evenly.

The vast majority of air fryers are outfitted with a variety of additional attachments that are designed to accommodate certain styles of cooking, such as grilling platters, pans for pizzas, cake barrels and skewer racks.

1.2 Advantages of Using an Air Fryer

People who use the Air Fryer may reap several health advantages as a consequence of its ability to generate outcomes that are comparable to those produced by deep-frying while using just a minute portion of the oil that is required for deep-frying.

During the process of deep-frying, the meal is first doused in oil, and it is this oil that is ultimately absorbed by the food, giving it a flavorful crust on the outside.

Although oil is still used in an air fryer due to its ability to brown and crisp a variety of meals, the amount of oil utilized is often restricted to one tablespoon at a time.

The meals are first thrown in the fryer with oil before being transferred to the basket of the air fryer. This eliminates the need to add the tablespoon of oil to the air fryer.

In point of fact, spraying the meals with oil in a light mist is an even simpler technique to guarantee that the foods have an equal coating while using the minimum quantity of oil possible.

Oil sprays, as opposed to oil drips, are an excellent method for ensuring that this is the case.

Swift and Low in Energy Consumption

It is not uncommon for conventional ovens to need fifteen to twenty mins of preheating time.

Due to the fact that the air fryer takes up so little space, the preheating process only takes two or three mins.

That will save a substantial amount of both time and power.

It is possible to preheat your air fryer without having to warm up the whole kitchen.

In addition to this,

You will save both time and energy since the strong heat inside the air fryer cooks food much more rapidly than it would in an oven—about 25 percent quicker, to be exact.

These days it seems like no one has any extra time, therefore the fact that this is available should make everyone happy.

Easy and Risk-Free

It is common knowledge that air-frying is a less dangerous and more user-friendly alternative to deep-frying.

The vast majority of air fryers are equipped with controls for adjusting both the duration and temperature of the cooking process.

That's about as simple as it gets, that's for sure!

When deep-frying, you were required to heat a big pan of oil on the stovetop and monitor the temperature using a deep-frying thermometer.

On top of everything else, you had a lot of responsibilities.

It was a really poor decision on your part to do that since oil is difficult to move, it may be hazardous if it gets too hot, and it is quite bothersome to drain and get rid of.

Ask yourself why you should go to the trouble of doing all that if you can get the identical outcomes in a manner that is far simpler with an air fryer.

Clear and in Order

It is imperative that you do not forget to put a little amount of water in the drawer below the bacon fat in order to prevent it from smoking.

In the end, the air fryer is a machine that is easy and uncomplicated to clean and maintain its cleanliness, and you are well aware of what they say about cleanliness...

Choosing Ingredients

You may find that you sometimes want to make use of your air fryer to prepare components of meals that may or may not really necessitate the use of an air fryer.

Toasting almonds for a salad in a short amount of time, roasting peppers for a pasta dish, or swiftly preparing bacon for an egg sandwich are all examples of time-saving preparation methods that should not be undervalued.

Recipes often call for certain ingredients to be prepared in a certain way, such as "toasted bread cubes" or "toasted walnuts," and the air fryer is there to save the day, once again helping you save time.

1.3 Suggestions for Making the Switch to a Diet Inspired by the Mediterranean

You don't need to be overwhelmed by the new eating habits that you will need to acquire in order to follow the Mediterranean diet if you are thinking of making a change in your lifestyle and adopting the Mediterranean diet.

Your diet will, for the most part, stay the same, with the exception of your consumption of unhealthy fats, foods that are too indulgent, and processed meals.

The following are some suggestions that can assist you in making the transition to a Mediterranean diet:

Eat a Lot of Fruits and Vegetables

Surprisingly, vegetables are also highly satisfying even though they may be cooked in various ways.

They will give you all of the minerals and vitamins that you need to keep your body in excellent condition, enhance your skin, cleanse your body, boost your mental moods, and keep your energy levels up throughout the day.

At every meal, vegetables may be prepared in a variety of ways, including chopping them up for a salad, blending them into a soup, or serving them as a side dish.

Always be sure you eat breakfast.

The first meal of the day, breakfast, is when you break your overnight fast and give your body a chance to start the day off on the right foot.

Consuming nutritious breakfasts that include fruits, whole grains, and other foods that are rich in fiber will not only provide you with the energy you need to get through the day but will also help you feel satisfied for a longer period of time.

Prepare at least one vegetarian dish every week in the kitchen.

Have you ever heard of the concept of "Meatless Mondays?"

This fad has been gaining popularity all around the globe in an effort to promote a way of life that does not rely on eating meat.

Even though meat is permitted on the Mediterranean diet, the high levels of saturated fat that are often present in meat products make it less desirable to consume it on a regular basis.

Try spending a day without eating meat and preparing your meals with legumes, nutritious grains, and veggies instead. This will give your body a chance to heal from the inside out.

When you feel like you have this under control, consider spending two days a week without eating any meat at all.

Moderate consumption of dairy products is recommended.

The United States Department of Agriculture (USDA) suggests limiting your consumption of saturated fats to no more than 10 percent of your daily calorie intake. Saturated fats are commonly found in meat and dairy products.

This suggests that the typical person should consume no more than 200 calories worth of saturated fats each day.

Because of this, you can consume dairy products like cheese and yogurt in reasonable quantities.

Enjoy Fruits As Dessert Options

The consumption of sweets is not forbidden when following a Mediterranean diet.

On the other hand, the dessert's risk of being harmful increases proportionately with the amount of sugar it contains.

There are situations in which a bowl of ice cream is suitable, but there are other situations in which you may choose a choice that is more beneficial to your health, such as fresh strawberry sorbet, frozen grapes, or apples that have been coated in honey.

Despite this, following a plant-based diet is just one component of the authentic Mediterranean diet.

In addition to this, it is important to engage in some kind of daily physical activity, such as walking or swimming, and to have meals with other people.

Your entire mood may be lifted and your stress level lowered when you participate in a meaningful conversation with others while eating a meal together.

In addition, dining with other people makes it more difficult to overeat since you are forced to share your food and engage in conversation in between bites.

The people of the Mediterranean region place a strong emphasis on the social aspects of food and utilize mealtime as an opportunity to strengthen bonds with loved ones and make new friends.

At the end of the day, interacting with others through food can help you manage your eating habits, enhance the connections you have with others, and improve your emotional, mental, and physical well-being. [Case in point:]

1.4 Delectable Fried Foods from the Mediterranean

If you were under the impression that adopting a Mediterranean way of life would require you to give up fried foods, you need revise your thinking.

It is now possible, thanks to the widespread dissemination of the air fryer, to concoct scrumptious dishes with a Mediterranean flavor that are not saturated in oil and do not pose a threat to one's wellbeing.

The reality is that the process of deep-frying food adds much more fat to the dish than does the preparation of the food using other ways of cooking.

For instance, a battered and deep-fried alternative to oven-roasted chicken breast includes 13.2 grams of fat for every 100 grams, whereas oven-roasted chicken breast comprises only 0.39 grams of fat per 100 grams.

Despite the fact that this information is available, many individuals would still choose to consume the chicken breast that has been deep-fried rather than the chicken breast that has been oven-roasted since the taste and texture of the former is superior to that of the latter.

Consuming fried food is no longer associated with feelings of guilt thanks to the invention of the air fryer, which employs an entirely new method to produce the same satisfyingly crunchy texture.

This makes it possible for those concerned about their health to enjoy fried dishes that have a lesser percentage of fat than those prepared in a deep fryer.

To get the same level of crispiness as deep-fried items, food is simply circulated about in an air fryer as it cooks.

The primary difference between air frying and traditional frying is that the former requires just a small percentage of the oil needed for the latter to get the same results in terms of taste and consistency.

To put it another way, the air fryer eliminates the use of oils that are heavy in both fat and calories from the process of frying dishes.

To get crispy chicken, sweet potatoes, or kale chips, all you need is one teaspoon of frying oil, as opposed to the many cups that are often required.

Air fryers, when used appropriately, have the potential to confer a number of positive health effects on its users.

To begin, it may assist in the reduction of excess body fat.

Those who often indulge in fried meals will have a lower calorie intake if they prepare their favorite fried dishes using an air fryer rather than a traditional deep fryer.

Second, as compared to conventional deep fryers, air fryers have a far lower risk of injury during usage.

To properly deep fry food, you must first bring a saucepan or pot filled to the brim with oil to a very high temperature.

When the oil becomes too hot, there is a good chance that it may spill or spatter over the cooktop, causing burns on anyone comes into contact with it.

Even though air fryers become rather hot, there is no danger of being burnt by the oil inside of them when you use them.

In spite of this, it is always advisable to follow the instructions in the air fryer handbook to ensure that the cooking process is both safe and easy.

In addition, if you cook meals using the conventional way of deep frying, you put yourself at risk of being exposed to harmful substances such as acrylamide, which may occur in some foods as a result of the process of deep frying.

For example, acrylamide has been associated with an increased risk of developing many forms of cancer, including ovarian, breast, endometrial, and pancreatic cancer.

By making the simple move to using an air fryer, you can significantly lower your exposure to acrylamide and other carcinogenic chemicals that are produced during the process of cooking at high temperatures.

1.5 Some Tips for Working with a Wide Variety of Oils and Fats

When you deep fried food, you generally use one kind of cooking oil or fat, but air frying allows you to utilize a larger range of oils and fats than you would normally use.

Because just a little amount of oil or fat is needed for air frying, you are free to use whatever combination of oils and fats you choose in the recipes you create for the technique.

If you have an air fryer with a basket, you may first melt the solid fats in the microwave before coating your food with them and putting it in the basket to cook. If you do not have an air fryer with a basket, you can simply skip this step.

When you are air-frying your favorite dishes, the following are some terrific healthy oil and fat alternatives that you may use:

Oil of Almonds

It is well knowledge that almond oil has a light taste of roasted almonds; however, this flavor is lost when the oil is heated.

Because of this, you should steer clear of using almond oil as your primary cooking oil.

Instead, you may put it to use as a flavored oil by adding it to the dish you are frying around five mins before it is done.

If you want to keep your almond oil fresh for as long as possible, you should keep it in the refrigerator, just as you would with any other nut-based oil.

Avocado Oil

When you air fried veggies like broccoli and green beans, adding avocado oil gives them a taste that is all their own.

Always keep your avocado oil in the refrigerator, and before using it in the air fryer, let it come to room temperature first. Avocado oil may be used to cook a variety of foods.

Coconut Oil

When added, foods prepared in an Asian manner benefit tremendously from the use of coconut oil.

When it is in its solid state, coconut oil may be substituted for butter in many recipes.

Before putting it into an air fryer to use it as oil, you should wait for it to reach room temperature or ensure that it still has the consistency of oil.

The olive oil

When applied to an air fryer, olive oil often evaporates very fast, despite the fact that it is a healthy cooking oil.

Because of how rapidly it is absorbed by some foods, such potatoes, mushrooms, and eggplant, you may need to add more than what the recipe calls for in order to get the desired results.

Duck Fat

When it comes to air frying meals, duck fat is one of the greatest cooking fats you can utilize.

This is due to the fact that a little amount of this component may go a very long way.

For instance, using one teaspoon of duck fat rather than three or four teaspoons of oil may effectively accomplish the same task.

To put it another way, if you cooked using duck fat, you would use less fat overall, which would result in a significant reduction in the number of calories you consumed.

You may keep the jar of duck fat in the refrigerator and then use a spoon to remove the fat from the jar whenever you need it.

Ghee

Ghee is a kind of clarified butter that lends a delicious flavor to dishes like risotto and curries when it is used in their preparation.

Ghee has a larger percentage of fat and more calories than butter does; nevertheless, a smaller amount of ghee goes a much longer way than butter does.

For instance, you would only need one tablespoon of ghee rather than two tablespoons of butter to do the same task.

Because of this, you will normally need less ghee than butter, and as a result, you will take in a lower total number of calories.

Goose Fat

Goose fat is another fantastic cooking fat that works well when used for air frying.

This is due to the fact that one tablespoon of goose fat is equivalent to three or four tablespoons of oil in terms of its functionality.

The goose fat that you have may be kept in the refrigerator, and whenever it is needed, you can simply take the quantity that you desire directly from the jar using a gentle scoop.

CHAPTER NO. 2
The Secret to Making Healthy Air-Fried Foods

Below are a few tips and suggestions for cooking high-quality crispy food and achieving the desired flavor and texture using your air fryer:

2.1 How to Achieve Even Cooking in an Air Fryer

The best way to achieve an even crispy coating on your foods is to avoid overfilling your air fryer. Hot air circulation can be compromised when there is too much food packed tightly together, causing the food to steam instead of frying evenly. When arranging your food in the air fryer, organize it in a puzzle formation, placing smaller pieces in the gaps between bigger pieces. When cooking protein, flip the meat or fish around half-way through cooking so that both sides receive an equal amount of heat. Avoid using your hands when flipping your meats as this may cause serious burns. Instead, use a pair of kitchen tongs for a quick and controlled grip.

2.2 How to Achieve Better Browning in an Air Fryer

To brown your meat and vegetables using an air fryer, simply pat the meat or vegetables down with a tea towel to remove excess moisture from the surface. Doing this will also prevent your food from steaming as it cooks, providing you with a crispier result. Cooking with fat can also help to brown your food in an air fryer. While many will try to avoid using fat, adding just a little to your food will produce tasty results! If you are not a fan of fat, you can substitute it with a little bit of honey. The sugar in the honey will aid in browning your meat or vegetables, as well as adding a great flavor. If you are cooking pastry dough in the air fryer, brush the dough with egg yolk before placing it in the fryer to give it a glossy brown coating when it has cooked through.

2.3 How to Achieve a Crunchier Coating Using an Air Fryer

One of the best tips that you can keep in your back pocket and use when air frying crispy chicken or vegetables, is to first pre-toast your bread or corn crumbs before coating your food with it. To pre-toast your bread or corn crumbs, drizzle a little oil on them and pop them in the microwave for a few mins. They should come out looking golden-brown and simply irresistible!

2.4 How to Cook Juicy Steaks in an Air Fryer

The first tip when cooking steaks in your air fryer is to cut them down in size so that you are able to fit more meat in your basket. After cutting your large steak pieces, add a seasoning or spice rub on each piece so that your meat is generously coated. Try to use seasonings that are darker in color and stronger in flavor to give your steak a better overall color and taste the cooking is complete.

2.5 How to Cook Fish in an Air Fryer

 The first tip when cooking fish in an air fryer is to cook it on a lower heat setting. While steaks can handle a blast of heat from an air fryer, your fish will come out looking and tasting a lot better on a lower heat. Fish will also require a longer time to cook through so that it is prepared in the most non-aggressive way. Cooking your fish on a low temperature for longer will also give it time to develop a crispy crust and the golden-brown color that we all love! You can also skewer your fish to allow for an easier removal out of the air fryer once it has been cooked. When air frying extremely delicate fish, place a sheet of foil on the base of the basket so that your fish does not stick to the bottom or break after cooking.

2.6 How to Cook Tender Chicken in an Air Fryer

 The number one tip for cooking chicken in an air fryer is to place your chicken pieces skin side up. This is because the heat in an air fryer comes from above. When turning your chicken pieces over, ensure that on the final turn the skin is facing up to give it the time to crisp in direct heat.

For even crispier and flavorful pieces of chicken, poke your meat with a skewer or fork to make a few holes in between the skin, allowing some of the chicken's oily juices to come out and brown the chicken even more.

2.7 How to Make Complete Meals Using an Air Fryer

Did you know that you can use an air fryer to prepare dinner from start to finish? There are a few tips on how to successfully do this. Firstly, learn how to stack your dinner in the air fryer. You can layer all of your dinner ingredients one on top of the other. For instance, placing vegetables directly under protein will allow the two to cook simultaneously and allow the oil juices from the meat to baste the vegetables below. More-over, use the microwave to prepare sauces or a simple side as your food cooks in the air fryer. The microwave can also be used to partially cook certain foods before being placed in the air fryer, thereby shortening the overall cook time.

CHAPTER NO. 3
Breakfast & Brunch

Try these recipes for breakfast and brunch;

3.1 Air Fryer Bagels

Servings: 4; **Preparation Time:** 5 min

Cooking Time: 10 min; **Total Time:** 15 min

Ingredients:

- 1 cup Plain Greek yogurt - zero-fat
- 1 cup Self-rising flour
- 1 Egg
- Desired Garnishes: Sesame or poppy seeds

Directions:

- Set the Air Fryer at 330° Fahrenheit ahead of baking time.
- Whisk the yogurt and flour to form a tacky dough.
- Dust a preparation surface and roll the dough into a ball, slicing it into four sections.
- Roll each one into bagel shapes and pinch to close. Prepare two at a time, brushing the tops with egg wash.
- Set the timer for ten mins after arranging the bagels in the cooker.
- For the toppings, brush with a portion of melted butter and season as desired.

Nutritional Facts: Cal: 123 Fat: 6.7 g Carbs: 7.3 g Protein: 9.8 g

3.2 Avocado Egg Boats

Servings: 2; **Preparation Time:** 6 min; **Cooking Time:** 12 min; **Total Time:** 18 min

Ingredients:

- 1 Avocado
- 2 Large eggs
- Optional Garnishes
- Freshly chopped chives
- Parsley
- Pepper

Directions:

- Set the Air Fryer temperature setting at 350° Fahrenheit.
- Discard the pit from the avocado. Slice and scoop out part of the flesh and add the seasonings.
- Break an egg into each half and place it in the Air Fryer. Set the timer for six mins.
- Serve using toppings of your choice.

Nutritional Facts: Cal: 114 Fat: 6.2 g Carbs: 5.1 g Protein: 5.8 g

3.3 Bacon-Wrapped Tater Tots

Servings: 4; **Preparation Time:** 7 min

Cooking Time: 9 min; **Total Time:** 16 min

Ingredients:

- 3 tbsp. Sour cream
- 1 lb. Medium-sliced bacon
- 1 large Bag of crispy tater tots
- 4 Scallions
- 5 cup Shredded cheddar cheese

Directions:

- Set the Air Fryer at 400° Fahrenheit.
- Wrap each of the tots in bacon and place them into the fryer basket. Keep them in a single layer.
- Set the timer for eight mins.
- Arrange the tots on a plate. Serve with the scallions and cheese garnish. Add a dash of sour cream.

Nutritional Facts: Cal: 120 Fat: 11.7 g Carbs: 4.2 g Protein: 9.6 g

3.4 Banana Fritters

Servings: 8; **Preparation Time:** 5 min

Cooking Time: 12 min, **Total Time:** 17 min

Ingredients:

- 3 tbsp. Vegetable oil
- 75 cup Breadcrumbs
- 3 tbsp. Corn flour
- 8 Ripe peeled bananas
- 1 Egg white

Directions:

- Warm the Air Fryer to reach 356° Fahrenheit.
- Use the low-heat temperature setting to warm a skillet. Pour in the oil and toss in the breadcrumbs. Cook until golden brown.
- Coat the bananas with the flour. Dip them into the whisked egg white and cover with the breadcrumbs.
- Arrange the prepared bananas in a single layer of the basket and place the fritter cakes onto a bunch of paper towels to drain before serving.

Nutritional Facts: Cal: 119 Fat: 8 g Carbs: 6.2 g Protein: 11.8 g

3.5 Easy Poached Eggs

Servings: 1, **Preparation Time:** 6 min

Cooking Time: 8 min; **Total Time:** 14 min

Ingredients:

- 3 cups Boiling water
- 1 Large egg

Directions:

- Set the Air Fryer at 390° Fahrenheit.
- Pour boiling water into the Air Fryer basket.
- Break the egg into a dish and slide it into the water. Set the basket into the fryer.
- Set the timer for 3 mins. When ready, scoop the poached egg into a plate using a slotted spoon.
- Serve with a serving of toast to your liking.

Nutritional Facts: Cal: 124 Fat: 6.2 g Carbs: 5.1 g Protein: 12.8 g

3.6 Easy Sausage Patties

Servings: 4; **Preparation Time:** 7 min

Cooking Time: 10 min; **Total Time:** 17 min

Ingredients:

- 12 oz. Pkg Sausage patties

Directions:

- Warm the Air Fryer at 400° Fahrenheit.
- Arrange the patties in a single layer, working in batches if needed.
- Set the timer for five mins.
- Flip the sausage over and cook until they reach 160° Fahrenheit on an instant-read thermometer or about three mins.

Nutritional Facts: Cal: 122 Fat: 11.3 g Carbs: 4.2 g Protein: 11.6 g

3.7 English Breakfast

Servings: 4; **Preparation Time:** 4 min

Cooking Time: 10 min; **Total Time:** 14 min

Ingredients:

- 8 Sausages
- 4 Eggs
- 8 Bacon slices
- 16 oz. can Baked beans
- 8 slices Toast

Directions:

- Arrange the bacon and sausage in the Air Fryer basket. Set the timer for ten mins at 320° Fahrenheit.
- Add the beans into a ramekin/heat-safe dish. In a second dish, add the whisked eggs.
- Increase the setting to 390° Fahrenheit.
- Place them in the basket and set the timer for another ten mins.
- Stir and serve when ready.

Nutritional Facts: Cal: 132 Fat: 15.3 g Carbs: 4.7 g Protein: 11.2 g

3.8 Grilled Cheese Sandwiches - Brunch

Servings: 2; **Preparation Time:** 7 min

Cooking Time: 12 min; **Total Time:** 19 min

Ingredients:

- 5 cup Sharp cheddar cheese
- 4 slices White bread or brioche
- 25 cup Melted butter

Directions:

- Set the Air Fryer at 360° Fahrenheit.
- Butter all slices of bread (both sides). Assemble each sandwich and arrange them in the fryer basket.
- Prepare for 5-7 mins and serve immediately for the best taste results.

Nutritional Facts: Cal: 134 Fat: 14.2 g Carbs: 4.6 g Protein: 16.6 g

3.9 Hawaiian Pizzas

Servings: 12; **Preparation Time:** 5 min;

Cooking Time: 12 min; **Total Time:** 17 min

Ingredients:

- 1 pkg Thomas' Light Multi-Grain English Muffins
- 1 cup Pizza sauce
- 5 cup Canadian Bacon
- 25 cup Crushed pineapple
- 1-2 cups Shredded mozzarella cheese

Directions:

- Set the fryer at 355° Fahrenheit.
- Gently, using your finger, separate the English muffins.
- Place a sheet of foil inside the Air Fryer,

making sure that air is still able to circulate. Spritz it with a non-stick cooking spray.

- Add the halves of the English muffins to the fryer (as many as can fit neatly).
- Top each half with sauce, Canadian bacon, and pineapple, and shredded cheese.
- Air-fry for 5 mins. It's essential to check them after about 3 mins to be sure all toppings are still cooking evenly.
- Remove and serve.

Nutritional Facts: Cal: 142 Fat: 22.3 g Carbs: 5.2 g Protein: 16.6 g

3.10 Mushroom Onion Cheese Frittata

Servings: 2; **Preparation Time**: 6 min

Cooking Time: 8 min; **Total Time**: 14 min

Ingredients:

- 1 tbsp. Olive oil
- 2 cups Mushrooms
- 1 small Onion
- 3 Eggs
- 50 g or 1/2 cup Grated cheese
- Also Needed: 1 Skillet

Directions:

- Warm the Air Fryer at 320° Fahrenheit.
- Prepare a skillet (medium heat) and pour in the oil.
- Chop the mushrooms and onions. Toss into the pan and sauté for about five mins before adding them to the Air Fryer.
- Whisk the eggs and salt. Dump it into the fryer with a sprinkle of cheese.
- Set the timer for 10 mins and remove to serve.

Nutritional Facts: Cal: 115 Fat: 6.2 g Carbs: 5.1 g Protein: 5.8 g

3.11 Pepperoni, Egg, and Cheese Pizza

Servings: 1; **Preparation Time**: 6 min

Cooking Time: 13 min; **Total Time**: 19 min

Ingredients:

- 5 tsp. Oregano
- 5 tsp. Basil
- 2 Eggs
- 2 tbsp. Shredded mozzarella cheese
- 4 pieces Thinly sliced pepperoni
- Also Needed: 1 ramekin

Directions:

- Whisk the eggs, basil, and oregano.
- Pour the eggs into the ramekin and add the pepperoni and cheese.
- Arrange the ramekin in the Air Fryer for three mins and serve.

Nutritional Facts: Cal: 120 Fat: 11.7 g Carbs: 5.2 g Protein: 9.6 g

3.12 Pumpkin Steel-Cut Oat

Servings: 4; **Preparation Time**: 5 min

Cooking Time: 11 min; **Total Time**: 16 min

Ingredients:

- 11/2 cups Water
- 5 cup Pumpkin puree
- 3 tbsp. Stevia
- 1 tsp. Pumpkin pie spice
- 5 cup Steel-cut oats

Directions:

- Heat the Air Fryer at 360° Fahrenheit to preheat.
- Toss in and mix the fixings into the Air Fryer.
- Set the timer for 20 mins.

- When it's ready, portion the oatmeal into bowls and serve.

Nutritional Facts: Cal: 119 Fat: 8 g Carbs: 6.2 g Protein: 11.8 g

3.13 Quick and Easy Doughnuts

Servings: 4; **Preparation Time**: 9 min

Cooking Time: 9 min; **Total Time**: 18 min

Ingredients:

- 1 can Flaky jumbo refrigerated dough biscuits
- 11/2 tsp. Ground cinnamon
- 5 cup White granulated sugar
- Coconut oil or ghee as needed

Directions:

- Set the Air Fryer at 350° Fahrenheit.
- Arrange the biscuits on a cutting board. Use a one-inch biscuit cutter to remove the centers.
- Grease the basket with the oil/ghee.
- Whisk the sugar and cinnamon.
- Air-fry the doughnuts for five to six mins. Fry the holes for three to four mins.
- Transfer to a dish and brush using the butter, garnishing using a sprinkle of the cinnamon/sugar mixture.

Nutritional Facts: Cal: 129 Fat: 8 g Carbs: 6.4 g Protein: 12.8 g

3.14 Raisin and Apple Dumplings

Servings: 2; **Preparation Time**: 5 min;

Cooking Time: 15 min; **Total Time**: 20 min

Ingredients:

- 2 tbsp. Raisins
- 2 Small apples
- 1 tbsp. Brown sugar
- 2 sheets Puff pastry
- 2 tbsp. Melted butter

Directions:

- Warm the Air Fryer to reach 356° Fahrenheit.
- Peel and core the apples. Combine the raisins and sugar. Place the apples on the pastry sheets and fill with the raisin mixture.
- Fold the pastry over to cover the fixings. Place them on a piece of foil so they won't fall through the fryer. Brush them with melted butter.
- Air-fry until they're golden brown (25 mins).
- Note: It's best to prepare using tiny apples.

Nutritional Facts: Cal: 122 Fat: 11.3 g Carbs: 4.2 g Protein: 11.6 g

3.15 Sausage Wraps

Servings: 8; **Preparation Time**: 5 min

Cooking Time: 10 min; **Total Time**: 15 min

Ingredients:

- 8-count can Crescent roll dough
- 2 slices American cheese
- 8 Heat and Serve Sausages
- 8 Wooden skewers
- Optional for Dipping: BBQ sauce/ketchup/syrup

Directions:

- Set the Air Fryer to 380º Fahrenheit.
- Open the sausages and separate the rolls.
- Slice the cheese into quarters and add the pieces starting on the widest part of the triangle to the tip. Add the sausage.
- Gather each end and roll-over the sausage and cheese. Pinch each side together. Add these in two batches to the fryer.
- Cook for 3-4 mins.
- Remove from the fryer and add a skewer. Set it out for serving with the desired garnish.

Nutritional Facts: Cal: 122 Fat: 11.3 g Carbs: 4.2 g Protein: 11.6 g

3.16 Scrambled Eggs

Servings: 1; **Preparation Time**: 6 min

Cooking Time: 12 min; **Total Time**: 18 min

Ingredients:

- Butter for the fryer basket
- 2 Eggs
- Black pepper as desired
- Optional: Cheese and tomatoes

Directions:

- Warm the Air Fryer at 285º Fahrenheit for about five mins.
- Melt a small portion of butter, spreading it out evenly.
- Whisk and dump the eggs and any other desired fixings desired.
- Open the fryer every few mins to whisk the eggs.
- Serve with a serving of toast or have a scrambled egg sandwich.

Nutritional Facts: Cal: 132 Fat: 15.3 g Carbs: 4.7 g Protein: 13.2 g

3.17 Spinach Frittata

Servings: 1-2; **Preparation Time**: 5 min

Cooking Time: 10 min; **Total Time**: 15 min

Ingredients:

- ⅓ of 1 pkg Spinach
- 1 small red onion
- Mozzarella cheese
- 3 Eggs

Directions:

- Heat the Air Fryer at 356º Fahrenheit for at least three mins.
- Pour the oil into a baking pan for one minute.
- Mince and toss in the onions. Sauté for two to three mins. Toss in the spinach and sauté another three to five mins.
- Whip in the eggs, add the seasonings, cheese, and add to the pan.
- Air Fry for 8 mins. Flavor with salt and pepper if you wish.

Nutritional Facts: Cal: 142 Fat: 13.2 g Carbs: 4.6 g Protein: 11.2 g

3.18 Egg Cups to Go

Servings: 4; **Preparation Time**: 6 min

Cooking Time: 10 min; **Total Time**: 16 min

Ingredients:

- 4 large eggs
- cup of diced veggies e.g., mushrooms, broccoli, tomatoes, peppers, spinach
- ½ of a cup of sharp cheddar cheese, shredded
- ¼ of a cup of half and half or light cream
- 2 tbsp. fresh coriander, chopped

Directions:

- Mix the eggs, veggies, half of the cheese, cream, and coriander together.
- Divide the mixture equally between 4 half-pint wide mouth jars (you can also use other pressure cooker-safe containers with lids).
- Put the lids on the jars – don't close them, as their job is only to prevent water from getting into the egg mixture.
- Add 2 cups of water into the Air fryer and place the trivet in.
- Then, put your jars carefully onto it.
- Set the timer for 5 mins and the pressure to the highest setting.
- Once it is done cooking, release the steam quickly.
- Carefully remove the jars from the cooker, sprinkle the tops of the eggs with the rest of the cheese and place the jars under a broiler (or into an air fryer) for additional 2-3 mins, or until the cheese is golden brown and bubbly.
- Add salt and pepper to taste.
- You can also garnish with herbs of your choice.

Nutritional Facts: Cal: 117 Fat: 8.7 g Carbs: 2.3 g Protein: 9.8 g

3.19 Eggs & Marinara

Servings: 4-6; **Preparation Time**: 8 min

Cooking Time: 12 min; **Total Time**: 20 min

Ingredients:

- 1 minced cloves of garlic
- 1 diced bell pepper, diced
- 1 ½ cup of sugar-free marinara sauce
- 4-6 eggs
- 2 tsp. paprika

Directions:

- Put some coconut oil into the Air fryer and set it to sauté.
- Once the oil is hot, carefully add the garlic and bell pepper.
- Sprinkle in the paprika and fry, stirring gently, for 5-6 mins – until the peppers soften.
- Pour in the marinara sauce and mix.
- Turn off the heat and let the mixture rest for another 5 mins.
- Make small, evenly spaced wells in the sauce with a back of a spoon and crack one egg into each well.
- Be careful to not break the yolks!
- After closing the lid – and making sure the valve is sealed – manually set the pressure to low and the timer to 5 mins.
- Once the timer beeps, carefully release the pressure valve and, once the steam has escaped, open the lid.
- Gently scoop out the eggs with the sauce.
- Sprinkle the top with freshly chopped parsley, add salt and pepper to taste and enjoy!

Nutritional Facts: Cal: 217 Total fat: 15.8 g Carbs: 6.7 g Protein: 10 g

3.20 Coconut Yogurt Parfait

Servings: 2; **Preparation Time**: 5 min

Cooking Time: 15 min; **Total Time**: 20 min

Ingredients:

- 2 cans of coconut cream
- 4 probiotic capsules (make sure they are allergen-free)
- 1 ½ tsp. of gelatin
- A mix of berries
- Pinch of cinnamon

Directions:

- Take two 1-pint mason jars and pour a can of coconut cream to each.
- Remember to shake the cans well before opening them.
- Sprinkle the insides of two probiotic capsules into each jar and mix them in well.
- Put the jars inside the Air fryer – leave them open, don't cover them, just secure the cooker's lid.
- Choose the Yogurt setting on the control panel and set the timer between 10 and 12 hours.
- The longer the yogurt incubates, the tarter it will become, so adjust the time to your preferences.
- After the time is up, remove the jars from the Air fryer and empty them into a blender.
- Add gelatin and blend thoroughly.
- Once the gelatin is mixed in, fill the jars back with the mixture and place the open jars in a fridge.
- Leave them there and cover with lids after a couple of hours.

- Once the yogurt is set, it is ready to be served.
- Mix it well first.
- Then, add a layer of it into a cup or a jar to cover the bottom.
- Place some of the berries on top and cover with another layer of yogurt and berries.
- Once your container is full, sprinkle a pinch of cinnamon on top and dig in!

Nutritional Facts: Cal: 142 Fat: 12.3 g Carbs: 4.1 g Protein: 21.2 g

3.21 Spinach & Tomato Quiche

Servings: 6; **Preparation Time**: 5 mins

Cooking Time: 20 mins ; **Total Time**: 25 mins

Ingredients:

- 12 eggs
- ½ of a cup of milk
- 2 cups of roughly chopped fresh spinach
- 1 cup of dices and seeded tomatoes
- ¼ of a cup of shredded cheese of your choice

Directions:

- Prepare your Air fryer – pour in 1 ½ cups of water and place the trivet in.
- Whisk the eggs and milk together in a bowl.
- Take a baking dish (1 and ½ quart is ideal), put the tomatoes and spinach in it and mix them gently together.
- Pour the egg and milk mixture over them and carefully stir it all together.
- You can also place thinly sliced tomatoes and some cheese over the top.
- With the help of a sling, place the dish onto the trivet.
- Close the lid and seal the valve of the pot.

- Set it to high pressure and set the timer for 20 mins.
- After the time is up, turn off the cooker and leave it as is.
- After 10 mins, quickly release the pressure and open the lid.
- Be careful of hot steam! Remove the pan from the pot and, if you want a golden-brown top, place it under a broiler for a few mins.
- When the quiche is done to your preference, salt, and pepper it to taste.

Nutritional Facts: Cal: 191.8 Fat: 10.6 g Carbs: 15.2 g Protein: 9g

3.22 German Pancakes

Preparation time: 10 minutes

Cooking time: 18 minutes

Total Time: 28 minutes **Servings:** 5

Ingredients:

- 1 cup oat flour
- 1/16 teaspoon salt
- 2 tablespoons olive oil
- 3 eggs
- 1 cup coconut milk, unsweetened
- Fresh berries, as needed for garnishing
- Swerve confectioners' sugar, as needed for garnish

Directions:

- Switch on the air fryer, insert fryer basket, then shut with its lid, set the fryer at 390 degrees F, and preheat for 10 minutes.
- Meanwhile, place all the ingredients in a blender, except for garnishing ones, and pulse until smooth; add 1 tablespoon of coconut milk if the batter is too thick.
- Take a heatproof ramekin, grease it with

olive oil, then pour in pancake batter and spread it evenly.

- Open the fryer, add ramekin in it, close with its lid and cook for 6 to 8 minutes until the pancake has cooked and the top is golden brown.
- When air fryer beeps, open its lid, take out the ramekin, then top with berries, and sprinkle with swerve confectioners' and serve.
- Nutrition: Calories: 139 Fat: 4 g Carbs: 18 g Protein: 8 g

Nutritional Facts: Cal: 191.8 Fat: 10.6 g Carbs: 15.2 g Protein: 9.7 g

3.23 Betty's Pancakes

Servings: 1; **Preparation Time:** 5 mins

Cooking Time: 45 mins; **Total Time:** 50 mins

Ingredients:

- 2 cups of coconut or almond flour
- 2 ½ tsp. of baking powder
- 2 tbsp. of low-carb granulated sweetener (e.g., Swerve, Sucralose, Xylitol)
- 2 large eggs
- 1 ½ cup of milk

Directions:

- Whisk the eggs and milk in a bowl until they are fully homogenous.
- In a separate bowl, thoroughly mix the rest of the ingredients.
- Combine them together and stir until you can see only small lumps.
- Lightly grease the Air fryer on the inside.
- Use a light oil (coconut works great) for best results.
- Pour the batter inside.
- Close the lid and secure the vent.

- Turn the pot into manual and set the pressure to low and time for 45 mins for a crispy pancake. You can decrease the time a little if you prefer a soft top.
- Once the time is up, release the pressure and test the pancake.
- When done, it should spring back when touched and not leave any raw batter on your finger. It will also release cleanly from the sides.
- Give it a little more time if needed, also on low pressure.
- Gently release the pancake from the pot with a knife or a spatula.
- Carefully remove it onto a plate upside down.
- Now what was the bottom of the pancake will be a beautifully golden brown and slightly crispy top!
- For final touches, add some toppings (make sure they are low carb) and enjoy!

Nutritional Facts: Cal: 149.2 Fat: 13.8 g Carbs: 3.6 g protein 4.7

3.24 Tofu Scramble

Preparation time: 10 minutes

Cooking time: 30 minutes

Total Time: 40 minutes **Servings:** 3

Ingredients:

- 4 cups broccoli florets
- 1 block tofu, drained, pressed, 1-inch cubed
- 2 1/2 cups chopped red potato, 1-inch cubed
- 1/2 cup chopped red onion
- 1/2 teaspoon garlic powder
- 1/2 teaspoon onion powder
- 1 teaspoon ground turmeric
- 2 tablespoons soy sauce
- 2 tablespoons olive oil

Directions:

- Place tofu pieces in a bowl, add onion, onion powder, garlic powder, and turmeric, drizzle with 1 tablespoon olive oil and soy sauce, toss until well coated, and set aside to marinate until required.
- Switch on the air fryer, insert fryer basket, grease it with olive oil, then shut with its lid, set the fryer at 400 degrees F, and preheat for 5 minutes.
- Meanwhile, place potato pieces in a bowl, add remaining oil and toss until well coated.
- Open the fryer, add potatoes pieces in it, close with its lid and cook for 15 minutes until nicely golden and crispy, shaking the basket every 5 minutes.
- Then add marinated tofu pieces into the fryer basket, shake well, reserving the marinade, and continue cooking for 10 minutes at 370 degrees F, shaking the basket every 5 minutes.
- In the meantime, add broccoli florets into the reserved marinade, toss until coated, and set aside until required.
- After 10 minutes of frying, add broccoli into fryer basket, shake well to mix and cook for 5 minutes
- When air fryer beeps, open its lid, transfer tofu, potatoes, and broccoli florets onto a serving plate and serve.

Nutrition: Calories: 276.3 Fat: 12.3 g Carbs: 29 g Protein: 13.1 g

3.25 Family Frittata

Servings: 4; **Preparation Time:** 10 mins

Cooking Time: 30 mins; **Total Time:** 40 mins

Ingredients:

- 4 large eggs
- 1 cup of light cream half and half
- 1 10-oz. can of green chilies (diced)
- ½ of a tsp. of ground cumin
- 1 cup of shredded Mexican cheese blend

Directions:

- Prepare a 6-inch pan – make sure it's air fryer-safe – by greasing the inside well (be thorough – eggs tend to stick!).
- Silicone or metal pans work best, as the frittata might need extra time if you use a glass one.
- In a bowl, whisk the eggs together with chilies, light cream (or half and half), ground cumin and about ½ of a cup of cheese.
- Pour the mix into the prepared tray and cover it with aluminum foil.
- Pour two cups of water into the air fryer, place in the trivet and gently lower the pan onto it.
- Close the valve and the lid, set the pressure to high and cook for 20 mins.
- Let the pressure come down naturally for ca. 10 mins, then release the rest quickly.
- Take out the pan and uncover it.
- Sprinkle the outstanding cheese over the surface and put the pan below a broiler.
- This should take about 5 mins, or until the cheese is golden and bubbly.
- You can finish the frittata with a sprinkling of salt and pepper, as well as some chopped fresh herbs of your choice – parsley works great. Enjoy!

Nutritional Facts: Cal: 254 Fat: 17.9 g Carbs: 5.7 g Protein: 13.8 g

3.26 Breakfast Biscuits

Preparation time: 10 minutes

Cooking time: 15 minutes

Total Time: 25 minutes **Servings:** 9

Ingredients:

- 1 cup almond flour
- 1/4 teaspoon sea salt
- 1/2 teaspoon baking powder
- 2 tablespoons butter, melted
- 2 tablespoons sour cream, non-fat
- 1 cup shredded cheddar cheese, non-fat
- 2 organic eggs

Directions:

- Place flour in a bowl, add salt and baking powder, stir until just mixed and then stir cheese by hand until incorporated.
- Crack eggs in another bowl, whisk in butter and sour cream until blended, and then slowly stir this mixture with a large fork until sticky batter comes together.
- Switch on the air fryer, then shut with its lid, set the fryer at 220 degrees F, and preheat for 5 minutes.
- Meanwhile, take a fryer basket, line it with parchment sheet, and then drop scoops of prepared biscuit batter in a single layer, about ¼ cup of batter for large biscuits or 2 tablespoons of batter for small biscuits.
- Open the fryer, insert fryer basket in it, close with its lid and cook for 10 minutes for large or 6 minutes for small biscuits until nicely golden and thoroughly cooked.
- When air fryer beeps, open its lid, transfer biscuits onto a serving plate and serve.

Nutrition: Calories: 167 Fat: 15 g Carbs: 3 g Protein: 7 g

3.27 French Toast Sticks

Preparation time: 10 minutes

Cooking time: 17 minutes

Total Time: 27 minutes **Servings:** 2

Ingredients:

- 4 slices of almond bread
- 1/16 teaspoon salt
- 1/16 teaspoon ground cloves
- 1/16 teaspoon ground cinnamon
- 1 teaspoon Swerve icing sugar
- 1/16 teaspoon nutmeg
- 2 tablespoons unsalted butter, softened
- 2 eggs, lightly beaten

Directions:

- Crack the eggs in a bowl, whisk until beaten, then add salt, cloves, cinnamon, and nutmeg, and whisk until mixed.
- Switch on the air fryer, insert fryer basket, grease it with olive oil, then shut with its lid, set the fryer at 350 degrees F, and pre-heat for 5 minutes.
- Meanwhile, spread butter on both sides of bread slices, cut the slices into strips and then dredge into the egg batter.
- Open the fryer, add bread strips in it in a single layer, spray with olive oil, close with its lid and cook for 6 minutes until nicely golden and crispy, flipping and spraying with oil halfway through.
- When air fryer beeps, open its lid, transfer French toasts onto a serving plate and cook remaining bread strips in the same manner.
- When done, sprinkle Swerve icing sugar on the French toasts and serve.

Nutrition: Calories: 178 Fat: 15 g Carbs: 2 g Protein: 5 g

3.28 Frittata

Preparation time: 10 minutes

Cooking time: 14 minutes

Total Time: 24 minutes **Servings:** 2

Ingredients:

- 1 ½ stick of waxed sausage, sliced length-wise
- ¼ cup chopped kale
- ¼ cup baby spinach leaves
- 2 tablespoons corn
- 1 tablespoon chopped red onion
- 2 tablespoons peas
- 1 small green bell pepper, cored, julienne cut
- 1 medium carrot, peeled, julienne cut
- 1/8 teaspoon salt
- 1/8 teaspoon ground black pepper
- ¼ teaspoon olive oil
- 3 eggs

Directions:

- Switch on the air fryer, then shut with its lid, set the fryer at 350 degrees F, and pre-heat for 5 minutes.
- Meanwhile, grease the air fryer baking pan, place sausage in it, add onion, stir until just mixed and spread evenly.
- Open the fryer, insert baking pan in it, close with its lid and cook for 4 minutes.
- Meanwhile, place the remaining ingredients in a bowl and whisk well until combined.
- When air fryer beeps, open its lid, pour in the prepared batter, and continue cooking for 4 minutes.
- Then increase air frying temperature to 390 degrees F and cook for 1 minute until the top of the frittata is nicely browned.

- When air fryer beeps, open its lid, take out the baking pan, transfer frittata onto a serving plate, then cut it into slices and serve.

Nutrition: Calories: 290.5 Fat: 19.7 g Carbs: 11 g Protein: 17.4 g

3.29 Breakfast Bombs

Preparation time: 10 minutes

Cooking time: 30 minutes

Total Time: 40 minutes **Servings:** 4

Ingredients:

- 4 ounces whole-wheat pizza dough
- 3 slices of bacon, center-cut
- 1 tablespoon chopped fresh chives
- 3 large eggs, beaten
- 1-ounce cream cheese, softened, low-fat

Directions:

- Take a skillet pan, place it over medium heat, add bacon, and cook for 10 minutes until very crispy.
- Then transfer bacon to a cutting board, let it cool for 3 minutes and then crumble it, set aside until required.
- Pour beaten eggs into the skillet pan, stir and cook for 1 minute until eggs are almost set.
- Transfer eggs into a bowl, add bacon, chives, and cream cheese and stir well until combined.
- Switch on the air fryer, insert fryer basket, grease it with olive oil, then shut with its lid, set the fryer at 350 degrees F, and preheat for 5 minutes.
- Meanwhile, divide pizza dough into four sections, roll each section into the 5-inch round crust, and then add one-fourth of the cooked egg mixture into the center of each crust.
- Brush the edges of the crust with water and then form a purse by wrapping crust around the egg mixture.
- Open the fryer, add crust in it in a single layer, then spray with olive oil, close with its lid and cook for 6 minutes until nicely golden brown.
- When air fryer beeps, open its lid, transfer the breakfast bomb onto a serving plate and cook the remaining crust in the same manner.
- Serve straight away.

Nutrition: Calories: 305 Fat: 15 g Carbs: 26 g Protein: 19 g

3.30 Air Fried Guacamole

Preparation time: 15 minutes

Cooking time: 16 minutes

Total Time: 26 minutes **Servings:** 10

Ingredients:

- 1/3 cup almond flour
- 1 egg
- 1 1/2 cups panko bread crumbs
- 1 egg white

For Guacamole:

- 3 medium avocados, halved, pitted, peeled
- 1/3 cup chopped cilantro
- 1/3 cup chopped red onion
- ½ teaspoon ground black pepper
- 2 teaspoons ground cumin
- 1 teaspoon of sea salt
- 8 tablespoons almond flour
- 1 lime, juiced

Directions:

- Prepare guacamole and for this, take a bowl, add all its ingredients in it except for flour and mash with a fork until well combined.
- Gradually mix the flour until thick and brownie dough-like batter comes together and freeze for 1 to 2 hours until the mixture has hardened.
- Meanwhile, take a baking sheet, and then line it with aluminum foil.
- After 2 hours, use a spoon to scoop out guacamole, shape it into a ball, and then place onto the prepared baking sheet.
- Prepare remaining guacamole balls in the same manner, cover the balls with aluminum foil, and then freeze for a minimum of 4 hours or overnight.
- Then switch on the air fryer, insert fryer basket, grease it with olive oil, then shut with its lid, set the fryer at 220 degrees F, and preheat for 5 minutes.
- In the meantime, crack the egg in a bowl, add egg white and whisk until combined.
- Place bread crumbs in a shallow dish and then place almond flour in another shallow dish.
- Working on one guacamole ball at a time, first spray the ball with oil, then coat with almond flour, dip into the egg mixture, then dredge with parmesan cheese and place the ball into heated fryer basket.
- Fill the fryer basket with more guacamole balls in the single layer, spray with olive oil, close with its lid and cook for 8 minutes until nicely golden and crispy, shaking the basket halfway through.
- When air fryer beeps, open its lid, transfer guacamole balls onto a serving plate, cook remaining guacamole balls in the same manner and serve.

Nutrition: Calories: 179 Fat: 13 g Carbs: 14 g Protein: 6 g

3.31 Bacon with Eggs

Preparation time: 5 minutes

Cooking time: 23 minutes

Total Time: 28 minutes

Servings: 1

Ingredients:

- 2 slices of bacon, thick-cut
- 2 eggs
- ¼ teaspoon salt
- ¼ teaspoon ground black pepper
- 2 tablespoons unsalted butter

Directions:

- Switch on the air fryer, insert fryer basket, grease it with olive oil, then shut with its lid, set the fryer at 400 degrees F, and pre-heat for 5 minutes.
- Then open the fryer, add bacon slices in it in a single layer, close with its lid and cook for 10 minutes until crispy and done, shaking the basket every 5 minutes.
- When air fryer beeps, open its lid, transfer bacon onto a serving plate and set aside until required.
- Replace fryer basket with air fryer baking pan, add butter in it, then shut with its lid, set the fryer at 400 degrees F, and cook for 1 minute until the butter has melted.
- Crack eggs in the baking pan, switch temperature to 325 degrees F, close air fryer with lid and cook for 6 to 8 minutes or until eggs are fried to the desired level.
- When air fryer beeps, open its lid, transfer fried eggs onto a serving plate and serve with bacon.

Nutrition: Calories: 487 Fat: 44.4 g Carbs: 1.2 g Protein: 20.7 g

3.32 Omelet

Preparation time: 5 minutes

Cooking time: 15 minutes

Total Time: 20 minutes

Servings: 1

Ingredients:

- 2 tablespoons chopped ham
- 2 tablespoons chopped red bell pepper
- 2 tablespoons sliced green onion
- 1 tablespoon chopped mushroom
- ¼ teaspoon salt
- 1 teaspoon breakfast seasoning
- 2 eggs
- ¼ cup coconut milk, unsweetened
- 2 tablespoons grated cheddar cheese
- 2 tablespoons grated mozzarella cheese

Directions:

- Switch on the air fryer, insert fryer baking pan, grease it with olive oil, then shut with its lid, set the fryer at 350 degrees F, and preheat for 5 minutes.
- Meanwhile, place crack eggs in a bowl, whisk them until beaten, then add ham, pepper, onion, mushrooms, and salt and whisk until just mixed.
- Open the fryer, pour in egg mixture, close with its lid and cook for 5 minutes.
- Then sprinkle breakfast seasoning on top, scatter with cheeses and continue cooking for 5 minutes until cheese has melted and omelet has cooked.
- When air fryer beeps, open its lid, take out the baking pan, slide omelet onto a serving plate and serve.

Nutrition: Calories: 350 Fat: 16 g Carbs: 19 g Protein: 6 g

3.33 Hash Browns

Preparation time: 30 minutes

Cooking time: 30 minutes

Total Time: 60 minutes **Servings:** 2

Ingredients:

- 1 small red onion, peeled, 1-inch sliced
- 1 1/2 pounds potatoes, peeled
- 1 medium red bell pepper, deseeded, 1-inch cubed
- 1 jalapeno, deseeded, cut into 1-inch rings
- 1/8 teaspoon salt
- 1/2 teaspoon ground cumin
- 1/8 teaspoon ground black pepper
- 1/2 teaspoon taco seasoning mix
- 1 1/2 tablespoon olive oil

Directions:

- Cut potatoes into 1-inch cubes, place them in a bowl, cover them with chilled water and let soak for 20 minutes.
- Then switch on the air fryer, insert fryer basket, grease it with olive oil, then shut with its lid, set the fryer at 320 degrees F, and preheat for 5 minutes.
- Meanwhile, drain the potatoes, pat dry with paper towels, place them in a bowl, drizzle with 1 tablespoon oil and toss until coated.
- Open the fryer, add potatoes in it, close with its lid and cook for 18 minutes until nicely golden, shaking the basket every 5 minutes.
- In the meantime, add onion, bell pepper, and jalapeno into the bowl that was used for potatoes, drizzle remaining oil over vegetables, season with salt, taco seasoning, black pepper, and cumin and toss until well coated.
- When potatoes are done, add them to the bowl containing vegetable mixture and toss until mixed.
- Return fryer basket into the air fryer, grease it with olive oil, then shut with its lid, set the fryer at 356 degrees F, and pre-heat for 5 minutes.
- Then open the fryer, add the vegetable mixture in it, close with its lid and cook for 12 minutes until nicely golden and crispy, shaking the basket every 5 minutes.
- When air fryer beeps, open its lid, transfer hash browns onto a serving plate and serve.

Nutrition: Calories: 186 Fat: 4.3 g Carbs: 4 g Protein: 4 g

3.34 Omelet with Herbs de Provence

Preparation Time: 10 minutes

Cooking time: 18 minutes

Total Time: 28 minutes **Servings:** 3

Ingredients:

- 6 eggs, beaten
- 1 tablespoon coconut milk
- 1 teaspoon Herbs de Provence
- 1 teaspoon coconut oil
- 1 oz Parmesan, grated

Directions:

- Grease the air fryer basket with coconut oil.
- Mix eggs with coconut oil and Herbs de Provence. Pour the liquid in the air fryer.
- Then top it with Parmesan and cook the meal at 365F for 18 minutes.

Nutrition: Calories: 181 Fat: 13.5g Carbs: 1.3g Protein: 14.2g

3.35 Egg and Spinach Muffins

Preparation Time: 10 minutes
Cooking time: 15 minutes
Total Time: 25 minutes **Servings:** 4
Ingredients:

- 1 cup Cheddar cheese, shredded
- 1 cup spinach, chopped
- 6 eggs, beaten
- 1 teaspoon coconut oil, melted
- 1 teaspoon dried oregano

Directions:

- In the mixing bowl, mix Cheddar cheese with spinach, eggs, and dried oregano.
- Brush the molds of the muffin with coconut oil and put the muffins mixture inside.
- Bake the muffins at 385F for 15 minutes.

Nutrition: Calories: 221 Fat: 17.1g Carbs: 1.4g Protein: 15.6g

3.36 Cayenne Pepper Eggs

Preparation Time: 10 minutes

Cooking time: 12 minutes

Total Time: 22 minutes **Servings:** 4

Ingredients:

- 1 teaspoon cayenne pepper
- 1 tablespoon butter, melted
- 8 eggs

Directions:

- Preheat the air fryer to 395F.
- Then brush the air fryer basket with butter and crack the eggs inside.
- Sprinkle the eggs with cayenne pepper and cook them for 12 minutes.

Nutrition: Calories: 153 Fat: 11.7g Carbs: 0.9g Protein: 11.2g

3.37 Garlic Zucchini Spread

Preparation Time: 10 minutes

Cooking time: 15 minutes

Total Time: 25 minutes **Servings:** 4

Ingredients:

- 4 zucchinis, roughly chopped
- 1 teaspoon garlic powder
- 1 tablespoon avocado oil
- ½ teaspoon salt

Directions:

- Mix zucchini with garlic powder, avocado oil, and salt.
- Put the mixture in the air fryer and bake at 375F for 15 minutes.
- Then blend the cooked zucchini until you get smooth spread.

Nutrition: Calories: 38 Fat: 0.8g Carbs: 7.3g Protein: 2.5g

3.38 Cream Cheese Rolls

Preparation Time: 15 minutes

Cooking time: 10 minutes

Total Time: 25 minutes; **Servings:** 4

Ingredients:

- 4 eggs, beaten
- ½ teaspoon coconut oil, melted
- ½ teaspoon chili flakes
- 2 tablespoons cream cheese

Directions:

- Mix eggs with chili flakes.
- Then brush the air fryer basket with coconut oil and preheat it to 395F.
- Make 4 crepes from egg mixture and cook them in the air fryer basket.
- Then spread the cream cheese over the every egg crepe and roll.

Nutrition: Calories: 85 Fat: 6.7g Carbs: 0.5g Protein: 5.9g

3.39 Honey-Apricot Granola With Greek Yogurt

Preparation time: 10 minutes

Cooking time: 30 minutes

Total Time: 40 minutes **Servings:** 6

Ingredients:

- Rolled oats - 1 cup
- Dried apricots - ¼ cup, diced
- Almond slivers - ¼ cup
- Walnuts ¼ cup, chopped
- Pumpkin seeds - ¼ cup
- Hemp hearts - ¼ cup
- Raw honey - ¼ to ⅓ cup, plus more for drizzling
- Olive oil -1 tablespoon
- Ground cinnamon - 1 teaspoon
- Ground nutmeg - ¼ teaspoon
- Salt - ¼ teaspoon
- Sugar-free dark chocolate chips - 2 tablespoons (optional)
- Nonfat plain Greek yogurt - 3 cups, for serving

Directions:

- Preheat the air fryer to 260F.
- Line the air fryer basket with parchment.
- In a bowl, combine everything except for yogurt and chocolate chips.
- Pour the batter into the air fryer basket. Spread in a single layer.
- Air Fry for 10 minutes. Then shake and Air Fry for 10 minutes more.
- Repeat the processes once more.
- Cool and stir in the chocolate chips.
- Serve with yogurt.

Nutrition: Calories: 342 Fat: 16g Carb: 31g Protein: 20g

3.40 Whole Wheat Banana-Walnut Bread

Preparation time: 10 minutes

Cooking time: 23 minutes

Total Time: 33 minutes **Servings:** 6

Ingredients:

- Cooking spray
- Ripe Bananas - 2
- Egg - 1
- Nonfat plain Greek yogurt - ¼ cup
- Olive oil - ¼ cup
- Vanilla extract - ½ teaspoon
- Raw honey - 2 tablespoons
- Whole wheat flour - 1 cup
- Salt -¼ teaspoon
- Baking soda - ¼ teaspoon
- Ground cinnamon - ½ teaspoon
- Chopped walnuts - ¼ cup

Directions:

- Preheat the air fryer to 360F.
- Coat a loaf pan with cooking spray.
- Mash the bananas in a bowl. Add the honey, vanilla, oil, yogurt, and egg. Mix until mostly smooth.
- Sift in the flour, cinnamon, baking soda and salt in the wet mixture. Stir until just combined. Careful not to overmix.
- Fold in the walnuts. Then pour batter into the loaf pan. Spread evenly.
- Air Fry in the air fryer for 20 to 23 minutes.
- Cool and serve.

Nutrition: Calories: 255 Fat: 14g Carb: 30g Protein: 6g

3.41 Mushroom-And-Tomato Stuffed Hash Browns

Preparation time: 10 minutes

Cooking time: 20 minutes

Total Time: 30 minutes **Servings:** 4

Ingredients:

- Cooking spray olive oil
- Olive oil - 1 tablespoon plus two teaspoons, divided
- Baby Bella mushrooms - 4 ounces, diced
- Scallion - 1, white parts and green parts, diced
- Garlic clove - 1, minced
- Shredded potatoes - 2 cups
- Salt - ½ teaspoon
- Black pepper - ¼ teaspoon
- Roma tomato - 1, diced
- Shredded mozzarella - ½ cup

Directions:

- Preheat the air fryer to 380F. Coat a cake pan with cooking spray.
- Heat 2 tsp. oil in a pan. Add garlic, scallion, and mushrooms. Cook for 5 minutes and remove from the heat.
- In a bowl, combine the remaining oil, salt, pepper, and potatoes. Coat well.
- Pour half of the potatoes into the pan and top with mozzarella, tomato, and mushroom mixture. Spread the remaining potatoes on top.
- Air Fry in the air fryer for 12 to 15 minutes.
- Remove, and cool. Slice and serve.

Nutrition: Calories: 164 Fat: 9g Carb: 16g Protein: 6g

3.42 Caprese Breakfast Pizza

Preparation time: 5 minutes

Cooking time: 6 minutes

Total Time: 11 minutes

Servings: 2

Ingredients:

- Whole wheat pita - 1
- Olive oil - 2 teaspoons
- Garlic clove - ¼, minced
- Egg - 1
- Salt - ⅛ teaspoon
- Tomato diced - ¼ cup
- Mozzarella pearls - ¼ cup
- Fresh basil leaves - 6
- Balsamic vinegar - ½ teaspoon

Directions:

- Preheat the air fryer to 380F
- Brush the top of the pita with oil. Then spread garlic on top.
- Break the eggs into a bowl and season with salt.
- Place the pita into the air fryer basket and pour in the egg on top of the pita.
- Top with basil, mozzarella pearls, and tomato.
- Air Fry for 6 minutes.
- Remove the pizza and drizzle with vinegar.
- Cool, slice and serve.

Nutrition: Calories: 209 Fat: 11g Carb: 19g Protein: 10g

3.43 Poached Eggs On Whole Grain Avocado Toast

Preparation time: 5 minutes

Cooking time: 7 minutes

Total Time: 12 minutes

Servings: 4

Ingredients:

- Cooking spray olive oil
- Eggs - 4
- Salt
- Black pepper
- Whole grain bread - 4 pieces
- Avocado - 4 pieces, chopped
- (Optional) Red pepper flakes

Directions:

1. Preheat the air fryer to 320F.
2. Coat four ramekins with cooking spray.
3. Break one egg in each ramekin. Then season with salt and pepper.
4. Air Fry in the air fryer for 7 minutes.
5. Meanwhile, toast the breads in the toaster.
6. In a bowl, add the chopped avocados, and season with red pepper flakes, black pepper, and salt. Mash the avocado lightly.
7. Spreads mashed avocado over each slice of toast.
8. Top with eggs and serve.

Nutrition: Calories: 232 Fat: 14g Carb: 18g Protein: 11g

3.44 Red Pepper And Feta Frittata

Preparation time: 10 minutes

Cooking time: 20 minutes

Total Time: 30 minutes

Servings: 4

Ingredients:

- Cooking spray olive oil
- Eggs - 8
- Red bell pepper - 1 medium, diced
- Salt - ½ teaspoon
- Black pepper - ½ teaspoon
- Garlic clove - 1, minced
- Feta - ½ cup, divided

Directions:

1. Preheat the air fryer to 360F.
2. Coat a pan with cooking spray.
3. Beat the eggs in a bowl.
4. Add the garlic, black pepper, salt, and bell pepper to the eggs. Mix.
5. Fold in ¼ cup of feta cheese.
6. Pour this mixture into the cake pan.
7. Sprinkle the remaining ¼ cup feta on top.
8. Air Fry in the air fryer for 18 to 20 minutes.
9. Cool and serve.

Nutrition: Calories: 204 Fat: 14g Carb: 4g Protein: 16g

CHAPTER 4:
Meal Options

Following are some meal options you can make for dinner and lunch:

4.1 Bacon-Wrapped Chicken

Servings: 3; **Preparation Time**: 3 mins

Cooking Time: 5 mins; **Total Time**: 8 mins

Ingredients:

- 1 Breast of chicken
- 6 strips of Unsmoked bacon
- 1 tbsp. soft garlic cheese

Directions:

- Slice the chicken into six portions.
- Spread the garlic cheese over each bacon strip. Add a piece of chicken to each one. Roll and secure with a toothpick.
- Prepare the Air Fryer ahead of fry time for about three mins.
- Arrange the wraps in the fryer basket. Air-fry them for about 15 mins.

Nutrition Facts: Cal: 206 Protein: 5g Carbs: 12g Fat: 8.4g

4.2 BBQ Chicken, Gluten-Free

Servings: 4; **Preparation Time**: 5 mins

Cooking Time: 10 mins; **Total Time**: 15 mins

Ingredients:

- 2 large Boneless - skinless chicken breast
- 5 cups Seasoned flour/Gluten-free seasoned flour
- 1 cup Barbecue sauce
- Olive oil cooking spray

Directions:

- Heat the Air Fryer to reach 390° Fahrenheit.
- Chop the chicken into bite-size chunks and place it in a mixing bowl.
- Coat the chunks with the seasoned flour.
- Lightly spritz the carrier of the Air Fryer with cooking spray and consistently pour the chicken into the cooker.
- Set the timer for 8 mins.
- Open the Air Fryer, coat the basket with olive oil spray, and flip the chicken as needed.
- Air-fry, the chicken for eight more mins. Be sure its internal reading is at least 165° Fahrenheit.
- Place the chicken into a dish and add the sauce.
- Line the Air Fryer with a sheet of foil or add the chicken back to the fryer and cook for another 3 mins until the sauce is warmed and the chicken is a bit crispier and more coated.
- Serve.

Nutrition Facts: Cal: 392 Protein: 23.3g Carbs: 5.9g Fat: 301/2g

4.3 Buffalo Chicken Wings

Servings: 2-3; **Preparation Time**: 10 mins

Cooking Time: 15 mins; **Total Time**: 25 mins

Ingredients:

- 1 tbsp. Butter - melted
- 5 /14 oz. Chicken wings
- 2 tsp. Cayenne pepper or to taste
- 2 tbsp. Red hot sauce
- 5 tbsp. Optional: Garlic powder

Directions:

- Heat the Air Fryer temperature to reach 356° Fahrenheit.
- Slice the wings into three sections end tip, middle joint, and drumstick.
- Pat each one thoroughly dry using a paper towel.
- Combine the pepper, salt, garlic powder, and cayenne pepper on a platter.
- Lightly cover the wings with the powder.
- Arrange the chicken onto the wire rack and bake for 15 mins, turning once at 7 mins.
- Combine the hot sauce with the melted butter in a dish to garnish the baked chicken when it is time to be served.

Nutrition Facts: Cal: 338 Protein: 18g Carbs: 1.8g Fat: 27g

4.4 Cheesy Chicken

Servings: 4; **Preparation Time**: 5 mins

Cooking Time: 15 mins; **Total Time**: 20 mins

Ingredients:

- 4 thin/2 breasts pounded Chicken breasts
- 1 cup Milk
- 1/2 cup Panko breadcrumbs
- 3/4 to 1 cup Shaved Parmesan-Asiago cheese blend
- Pepper as desired

Directions:

- Set the Air Fryer temperature at 400° Fahrenheit. Lightly spritz the basket with a non-stick cooking oil spray.
- Add the milk, chicken, and pepper into a bowl to marinate for about ten mins.
- Prepare a shallow dish with the breadcrumbs and cheese.
- Dredge the chicken through the mixture and place it in the basket of the fryer.
- Cook it in batches, lightly spraying the tops with the oil spray.
- Set the timer for eight mins and flip the breasts about halfway through the cycle at four mins.
- Reheat the first batch for about one minute if desired and serve.

Nutrition Facts: Cal. 191.8 Fat: 10.6 g Carbs: 15.2 g Protein: 9.7 g

4.5 Chicken Breast Tenderloins

Servings: 4; **Preparation Time**: 10 mins

Cooking Time: 20 mins; **Total Time**: 30 mins

Ingredients:

- 2 tbsp. Butter/vegetable oil
- 3 tbsp. Breadcrumbs
- 1 Egg
- 8 Chicken tenderloins

Directions:

- Heat the Air Fryer temperature to 356° Fahrenheit.
- Combine the breadcrumbs and oil - stirring until the mixture crumbles.
- Whisk the egg and dredge the chicken through the egg, shaking off the excess.
- Dip each piece of chicken into the crumbs and evenly coat.
- Set the timer for 12 mins.

Nutrition Facts: Cal. 191.8 Fat: 10.6 g Carbs: 15.2 g Protein: 9.7 g

4.6 Chicken Fillet Strips

Servings: 4; **Preparation Time**: 5 mins

Cooking Time: 20 mins; **Total Time**: 25 mins

Ingredients:

- 1 lb. Chicken fillets
- 1 tbsp. Paprika
- 1 tbsp. Heavy cream
- 1/2 tbsp. Black pepper
- Butter as needed

Directions:

- Heat the Air Fryer at 365° Fahrenheit.
- Slice the fillets into strips and dust with salt and pepper.
- Add a light coating of butter to the basket.
- Arrange the strips in the basket and air-fry

for six mins.

- Flip the strips and continue frying for another five mins.
- When done, garnish with the cream and paprika. Serve warm.

Nutrition Facts: Cal: 240 Protein: 13.9g Carbs: 2.7g Fat: 19.4g

4.7 Chinese Chicken Wings

Servings: 2; **Preparation Time**: 10 mins

Cooking Time: 15 mins; **Total Time**: 25 mins

Ingredients:

- 4 Chicken wings
- 1 tbsp. Chinese spice
- 1 tbsp. Mixed spices - your choice
- 1 tbsp. Soy sauce

Directions:

- Warm the Air Fryer to 356° Fahrenheit.
- Add the seasonings into a large mixing bowl, stirring thoroughly.
- Pour it over the chicken wings until each piece is covered.
- Put some aluminum foil on the base of the fryer and add the chicken sprinkling any remnants over the chicken. Air-fry it for 15 mins.
- Flip the chicken and air-fry for another 15 mins at 392° Fahrenheit.

Nutrition Facts: Cal: 392 Protein: 23.3g Carbs: 5.9g Fat: 301/2g

4.8 Chicken Bits

Servings: 4; **Preparation Time**: 6 mins

Cooking Time: 14 mins; **Total Time**: 20 mins

Ingredients:

- 4 thin/2 breasts pounded Chicken breasts
- 1 cup Milk
- 1/2 cup Panko breadcrumbs
- 3/4 to 1 cup Shaved Parmesan-Asiago cheese blend
- Pepper as desired

Directions:

- Set the Air Fryer temperature at 400° Fahrenheit.
- Lightly spritz the basket with a non-stick cooking oil spray.
- Add the milk, chicken, and pepper into a bowl to marinate for about ten mins.
- Prepare a shallow dish with the bread-crumbs and cheese.
- Dredge the chicken through the mixture and place it in the basket of the fryer.
- Cook it in batches, lightly spraying the tops with the oil spray.
- Set the timer for eight mins and flip the breasts about halfway through the cycle at four mins.
- Reheat the first batch for about one minute if desired and serve.

Nutritional Facts: Cal: 125 Fat: 1.2 g Carbs: 0.1 g Protein: 27 g

4.9 Coconut-Crusted Chicken Tenders

Servings: 4; **Preparation Time**: 10 mins

Cooking Time: 15 mins; **Total Time**: 25 mins

Ingredients:

- 3 Eggs
- 1 lb. Chicken tenders
- 1 cup Cornstarch
- 2 cups Sweetened shredded coconut
- 1 tsp. Cayenne pepper

Directions:

- Set the Air Fryer temperature at 360° Fahrenheit.
- Prepare three dishes. In the first one, add the cornstarch and cayenne with any other desired seasonings. In the second bowl, add the eggs.
- Lastly, add the coconut in the third dish.
- Dredge the chicken through the corn-starch, egg, and coconut.
- Lightly spritz the fryer basket with a cooking oil spray as needed.
- Set the timer for 8 mins on the air-fry until its golden brown before serving.

Nutrition Facts: Cal: 392 Protein: 23.3g Carbs: 5.9g Fat: 301/2g

4.10 Crispy Chicken Sliders

Servings: 6 = 12 sliders; **Prep Time:** 15 mins

Cooking Time: 25 mins; **Total Time:** 40 mins

Ingredients:

- 1 pkg. Tyson Crispy Chicken Strips
- 1 pkg. Sweet Hawaiian Rolls
- Optional Ingredients:
- Spinach leaves
- Tomatoes
- Honey mustard

Directions:

- Place the six chicken strips in the Air Fryer basket with a coating of olive oil spray.
- Cook at 390° Fahrenheit for 8 mins.
- Cut the rolls in half and highest them with honey mustard, tomatoes and spinach or other toppings of your choice.
- Slice the chicken strips into chunks and place them on the rolls.

Nutrition Facts: Cal. 191.8 Fat: 10.6 g Carbs: 15.2 g Protein: 9.7 g

4.11 Garlic Herb Turkey Breast

Servings: 6; **Preparation Time:** 10 mins

Cooking Time: 45 mins; **Total Time:** 55 mins

Ingredients:

- 2 lb. Turkey breast
- 4 tbsp. Melted butter
- 3 cloves Garlic
- 1 tsp. Thyme
- 1 tsp. Rosemary

Directions:

- Warm the Air Fryer to reach 375° Fahrenheit.
- Pat the turkey breast dry. Mince the garlic

and chop the rosemary and thyme.

- Melt the butter and mix with the garlic, thyme, and rosemary in a small mixing bowl. Brush the butter over turkey breast.
- Place in the Air Fryer basket, skin side up, and cook for 40 mins or until internal temperature reaches 160° Fahrenheit, flipping halfway through.
- Wait for five mins before slicing.

Nutrition Facts: Cal: 240 Protein: 13.9g Carbs: 2.7g Fat: 19.4g

4.12 Honey-Lime Chicken Wings

Servings: 4; **Preparation Time:** 10 mins

Cooking Time: 20 mins; **Total Time:** 30 mins

Ingredients:

- 2 lb. Chicken wings
- 2 tbsp. Lime juice
- 1/4 cup Honey
- 1 tbsp. Lime zest
- 1 pressed Garlic clove

Directions:

- Warm the Air Fryer at 360° Fahrenheit.
- Whisk the garlic, honey, and lime juice and zest.
- Toss in the wings and cover with the mixture.
- Prepare the wings in batches. Cook for 25-30 mins until they're crispy.
- Shake the basket at 8-minute intervals.
- Serve and garnish as desired.

Nutrition Facts: Cal: 392 Protein: 23.3g Carbs: 5.9g Fat: 301/2g

4.13 Rotisserie-Style, Whole Chicken

Servings: 4; **Preparation Time:** 5 mins

Cooking Time: 60 mins; **Total Time:** 65 mins

Ingredients:

- 2 tsp. or as needed Olive oil
- 6-7 lb. Whole chicken
- 1 tbsp. Seasoned salt

Directions:

- Set the Air Fryer at 350° Fahrenheit.
- Coat the chicken with oil and a sprinkle of salt.
- Arrange the chicken in the Air Fryer – skin-side down.
- Cook for 30 mins. Flip the chicken over and air-fry for another 30 mins.
- Wait for ten mins before slicing
- Note: This recipe is for chickens under 6 lb. for a 3.7-quart Air Fryer.

Nutrition Facts: Cal: 392 Protein: 23.3g Carbs: 5.9g Fat: 301/2g

4.14 Air Fryer Chicken Parmesan

Preparation Time: 15 minutes

Cooking Time: 9 minutes

Total Time: 24 minutes

Servings: 4

Ingredients:

- ½ C. keto marinara
- 6 tbsp mozzarella cheese
- 1 tbsp melted ghee
- 2 tbsp grated parmesan cheese
- 6 tbsp gluten-free seasoned breadcrumbs
- 2 8-ounce chicken breasts

Directions:

- Ensure air fryer is preheated to 360 degrees. Spray the basket with olive oil.
- Mix parmesan cheese and breadcrumbs together. Melt ghee.
- Brush melted ghee onto the chicken and dip into breadcrumb mixture.
- Place coated chicken in the air fryer and top with olive oil.
- Cook 2 breasts for 6 minutes and top each breast with a tablespoon of sauce and 1 ½ tablespoons of mozzarella cheese. Cook another 3 minutes to melt cheese.
- Keep cooked pieces warm as you repeat the process with remaining breasts.

Nutrition: Calories 251 Fat 10g Protein 31g Carbs: 0g

4.15 Chance's Chicken

Servings: 6/8; **Preparation Time:** 2 mins

Cooking Time: 8 minS; **Total Time:** 10 mins

Ingredients:

- 4 pounds of skinless, boneless chicken breast
- ½ of a tsp. of sea salt
- ½ of a tsp. of ground black pepper
- 1 tbsp. of Italian seasoning pre-mixed
- 1 cup of chicken broth

Directions:

- Season the chicken breasts generously on both sides with sea salt, pepper, and Italian seasoning.
- You can also use other spices and herbs of your choice.
- Place the breasts inside the Air fryer and carefully pour in the broth. Pour around the meat as to not wash off the seasonings.
- Secure the lid and choose the Poultry setting or Manual on the control panel.
- For breasts that are about 6-8 ounces, the cooking time is 8 mins for fresh and 13 mins for frozen meat.
- If your chicken breasts are smaller or

larger than that, tweak the time as needed.

- After the time is up, let the pressure release on its own – this will yield the tenderest meat.
- If you are pressed for time, allow the natural release for 5-7 mins and then release the rest quickly.
- You can now unplug the air fryer and start shredding the chicken.
- Work with two forks.
- You can take the breasts out but shredding them inside the pot will make them juicier as they mix with the broth. If you want to serve the chicken immediately, allow it to drain for a bit, but in can be stored in the broth for later – it will help it stay moist.

Nutrition Facts: Cal: 240 Protein: 13.9g Carbs: 2.7g Fat: 19.4g

4.16 Chicken Chili Verde

Servings: 6; **Preparation Time**: 5 mins

Cooking Time: 25 mins; **Total Time**: 30 mins

Ingredients:

- 2 pounds of chicken breasts or thighs
- ½ of a tsp. of cumin, ground
- ¼ of a tsp. of garlic powder
- 16 ounces of salsa Verde
- Salt and pepper, to taste

Directions:

- Place the chicken meat inside the cooker. Sprinkle with seasonings and pour the salsa on top.
- Set the pressure to high and cook for 25 mins.
- After that time, release the pressure quickly. Using two forks, shred the meat inside the pot and mix with the juices and

salsa. Taste for seasoning and adjust as necessary.

Nutritional Facts: Cal. 206 Total fat: 4.8 g Total Carbs: 3.9 g Proteins: 33 g

4.17 Chicken & Salsa

Servings: 4; **Preparation Time**: 5 mins

Cooking Time: 8 minS; **Total Time**: 13 mins

Ingredients:

- 2 tbsp. of taco seasoning
- 1 cup of salsa
- 3 medium-sized chicken breasts

Directions:

- Pour a little avocado oil into the bottom of the air fryer. Set it to sauté and let the oil heat.
- In the meantime, rub the breasts thoroughly with the taco seasoning on both sides.
- Place the meat inside the pot and let it brown for 1-2 mins on each side. Don't cook the chicken through!
- Cover the chicken with salsa and close the lid. Set the pressure to high and cook for 5 mins.
- Let the pressure release on its own for 5-7 mins when the time is up. Release the residual pressure quickly and open the lid.
- Shred the meat using two forks, mix it with the juices and salsa and let it sit for a bit, so it absorbs the delicious flavors.
- You can serve the meat with Greek yogurt – and enjoy!
- NOTE: Lettuce makes a great substitute for taco shells, too!

Nutritional Facts: Cal: 148 Total Fat: 6.8 g Carbs: 11.7 g Protein: 10 g

4.18 Jerk Chicken Wings

Preparation Time: 10 minutes

Cooking Time: 16 minutes

Total Time: 26 minutes

Servings: 8

Ingredients:

- 1 tsp. salt
- ½ C. red wine vinegar
- 5 tbsp lime juice
- 4 chopped scallions
- 1 tbsp grated ginger
- 2 tbsp brown sugar
- 1 tbsp chopped thyme
- 1 tsp. white pepper
- 1 tsp. cayenne pepper
- 1 tsp. cinnamon
- 1 tbsp allspice
- 1 Habanero pepper (seeds/ribs removed and chopped finely)
- 6 chopped garlic cloves
- 2 tbsp low-Sodium soy sauce
- 2 tbsp olive oil
- 4 pounds of chicken wings

Directions:

- Combine all ingredients except wings in a bowl. Pour into a gallon bag and add chicken wings. Chill 2-24 hours to marinate.
- Ensure your air fryer is preheated to 390 degrees.
- Place chicken wings into a strainer to drain excess liquids.
- Pour half of the wings into your air fryer and cook 14-16 minutes, making sure to shake halfway through the cooking process.
- Remove and repeat the process with remaining wings.

Nutrition: Calories 374 Fat 14g Protein 33g

Carbs: 4g

4.19 Keto Chicken Wings

Servings: 6; **Preparation Time:** 7 mins

Cooking Time: 22 minS; **Total Time:** 29 minS

Ingredients:

- 5 pounds of chicken wings
- 1 cup of hot sauce use the one you like for optimal spiciness
- ¼ of a cup of apple cider vinegar
- 1 tbsp. of clarified butter or ghee
- 1 tsp. each of sea salt and ground black pepper

Directions:

- In a bowl, whisk together the vinegar, melted ghee, hot sauce, salt, and pepper.
- Save ¼ of a cup to baste the wings and glaze them. (remove the wing tips)
- Place the wings inside the inner pot of the pressure cooker, pour over the hot sauce mix and stir them together, making sure the wings are well covered.
- Once you're ready to cook, turn the Air fryer on, put the inner pot inside and close the lid and the valve. Set for manual cooking and set the timer for 10 mins.
- As the wings are cooking, prepare your oven by setting it to broiling and line a cookie sheet with parchment or baking paper.
- When the time is up, allow the pressure to release on its own.
- Open the lid when the float valve of the event is open – this will take about 10 to 12 mins.
- Carefully open the lid, take the wings out and transfer them to the lined baking sheet. Make sure they are evenly spread and lie flat on it.
- Baste them with the extra hot sauce mix

you saved up earlier.

- Place the sheet with wings under the broiler.
- Let the wings become brown but be careful not to burn the skin.
- It should take about 4-6 mins, after which you can turn the wings to the other side to broil.
- Once they're done, take them out and arrange them on a platter.
- Immediately before serving, drizzle them with a little more sauce.
- Serve your wings immediately with extra dips or sauces and the garnishes you like.

Nutritional Facts: Cal: 937 Carbs: 0.9 g Protein: 68 g Fat: 68.9 g

4.20 Chicken Cacciatore

Servings: 4; **Preparation Time**: 10 mins

Cooking Time: 35 minuS; **Total Time**: 45 mins

Ingredients:

- 4 boneless, skinless chicken thighs
- ½ of a 14-ounce can crushed tomatoes
- ½ of a cup of diced onion
- 1/2 cup each of diced green and red bell pepper
- 1 bay leaf

Directions:

- Set your air fryer to sauté and add a little oil to the bottom.
- Season the thighs generously on both sides with salt and pepper and place them on the hot oil to brown.
- When both sides are browned, remove the meat and set it aside.
- Add a little more oil to the pot and put the peppers and onion inside.
- Sauté them for about 5 mins until they soften up.

- Put the chicken thighs back into the pot, pour the tomatoes over them and mix everything together well.
- Then, close the lid and set the pressure to high.
- Cook for 25 mins, and after that time allow the pressure to release naturally.
- Take the bay leaf out before serving, sprinkle some fresh oregano and parsley over the top and serve with your favorite sides make them low carb!

Nutritional Facts: Cal: 131 Carbs: 10.3 g Protein: 13.8 g Fat: 2.9 g

4.21 Korean Chicken Wings

Preparation Time: 10 minutes

Cooking Time: 25 minutes

Total Time: 35 minutes

Servings: 4

Ingredients:

- Wings:
- 1 tsp. pepper
- 1 tsp. salt
- 2 pounds' chicken wings
- Sauce:
- 2 packets Splenda
- 1 tbsp minced garlic
- 1 tbsp minced ginger
- 1 tbsp sesame oil
- 1 tsp. agave nectar
- 1 tbsp mayo
- 2 tbsp gochujang
- Finishing:
- ¼ C. chopped green onions
- 2 tsp. sesame seeds

Directions:

- Ensure air fryer is preheated to 400 degrees.
- Line a small pan with foil and place a rack

onto the pan, then place into air fryer.

- Season the wings with pepper and salt and place onto the rack.
- Air fry 20 minutes, turning at 10 minutes
- As chicken air fries, mix together all the sauce components.
- Once a thermometer says that the chicken has reached 160 degrees, take out wings and place into a bowl.
- Pour half of the sauce mixture over wings, tossing well to coat.
- Put coated wings back into air fryer for 5 minutes or till they reach 165 degrees.
- Remove and sprinkle with green onions and sesame seeds. Dip into extra sauce.

Nutrition: Calories 356 Fat 26g Protein 23g Carbs: 2g

4.22 Buffalo Chicken Wings

Preparation Time: 15 minutes

Cooking Time: 30 minutes

Total Time: 45 minutes

Servings: 8

Ingredients:

- 1 tsp. salt
- 1-2 tbsp brown sugar
- 1 tbsp Worcestershire sauce
- ½ C. vegan butter
- ½ C. cayenne pepper sauce
- 4 pounds' chicken wings

Directions:

- Whisk salt, brown sugar, Worcestershire sauce, butter, and hot sauce together and set to the side.
- Dry wings and add to air fryer basket.
- Cook 25 minutes at 380 degrees, tossing halfway through.

- When timer sounds, shake wings and bump up the temperature to 400 degrees and cook another 5 minutes
- Take out wings and place into a big bowl. Add sauce and toss well.
- Serve alongside celery sticks!

Nutrition: Calories 402 Fat 16g Protein 17g Carbs: 4g

4.23 Shredded Chicken

Servings: 4; **Preparation Time:** 30 mins

Cooking Time: 47 mins; **Total Time:** 73 mins

Ingredients:

- 4 pounds of chicken breasts
- ½ of a cup of chicken broth or water
- 1 tsp. of sea salt
- ½ tsp. of ground black pepper

Directions:

- Place your ingredients in the Air fryer together.
- Close the lid and select the poultry setting.
- Let them cook for 5 mins.
- If you are using frozen tenders, increase the time to 10 mins, and to 15 mins for frozen breasts.
- After the timer beeps, release the valve and quickly depressurize the pot.
- Remove the chicken and let it test on a board or a plate for a couple of mins, then shred it.
- It can be stored in an airtight container, covered in some of the juices from the pot.

Nutritional Facts: Cal: 125 Fat: 1.2 g Carbs: 0.1 g Protein: 27 g

4.24 Chicken Fajita Rollups

Preparation Time: 5 minutes

Cooking Time: 12 minutes

Total Time: 17 minutes

Servings: 8

Ingredients:

- ½ tsp. oregano
- ½ tsp. cayenne pepper
- 1 tsp. cumin
- 1 tsp. garlic powder
- 2 tsp. paprika
- ½ sliced red onion
- ½ yellow bell pepper, sliced into strips
- ½ green bell pepper, sliced into strips
- ½ red bell pepper, sliced into strips
- 3 chicken breasts

Directions:

- Mix oregano, cayenne pepper, garlic powder, cumin and paprika along with a pinch or two of pepper and salt. Set to the side.
- Slice chicken breasts lengthwise into 2 slices.
- Between two pieces of parchment paper, add breast slices and pound till they are ¼-inch thick. With seasoning liberally season both sides of chicken slices.
- Put 2 strips of each color of bell pepper and a few onion slices onto chicken pieces.
- Roll up tightly and secure with toothpicks.
- Repeat with remaining ingredients and sprinkle and rub mixture that is left over the chicken rolls.
- Lightly grease your air fryer basket and place 3 rollups into the fryer. Cook 12 minutes at 400 degrees.
- Repeat with remaining rollups.
- Serve with salad!

Nutrition: Calories 189 Fat 14g Protein 11g

Carbs: 1g

4.25 Coconut Turmeric Chicken

Servings: 4; **Preparation Time**: 2 mins

Cooking Time: 15 mins; **Total Time**: 17 mins

Ingredients:

- 2 pounds of skinless, boneless chicken thighs
- 1 can of coconut cream
- 1 tbsp. of turmeric

Directions:

- Place the thighs in the Air fryer, add the coconut cream and turmeric.
- Gently mix everything together until it's combined.
- Choose the poultry setting on your cooker, set the pressure to high and the timer to 15 mins.
- Release the pressure quickly after that time, taste for seasoning add salt and pepper as needed and serve alongside your preferred side dishes!

Nutritional Facts: Cal: 321 Fat: 11.8 g Carbs: 8.8 g Proteins: 45 g

4.26 Crispy Honey Garlic Chicken Wings

Preparation Time: 15 minutes

Cooking Time: 35 minutes

Total Time: 50 minutes

Servings: 8

Ingredients:

- 1/8 C. water
- ½ tsp. salt
- 4 tbsp minced garlic
- ¼ C. vegan butter
- ¼ C. raw honey
- ¾ C. almond flour
- 16 chicken wings

Directions:

- Rinse off and dry chicken wings well.
- Spray air fryer basket with olive oil.
- Coat chicken wings with almond flour and add coated wings to air fryer. Cook 25 minutes at 380 degrees, shaking every 5 minutes
- When the timer goes off, cook 5-10 minutes at 400 degrees till skin becomes crispy and dry.
- As chicken cooks, melt butter in a saucepan and add garlic. Sauté garlic 5 minutes Add salt and honey, simmering 20 minutes Make sure to stir every so often, so the sauce does not burn. Add a bit of water after 15 minutes to ensure sauce does not harden.
- Take out chicken wings from air fryer and coat in sauce. Enjoy!

Nutrition: Calories 435 Fat 19g Protein 31g Carbs: 6g

4.27 Rosemary Turkey Breast with Maple Mustard Glaze

Preparation Time: 20 minutes

Cooking Time: 30 minutes

Total Time: 50 minutes

Servings: 7

Ingredients:

- 1 tbsp vegan butter
- 1 tbsp stone-ground brown mustard
- ¼ C. pure maple syrup
- 1 tsp. crushed pepper
- 2 tsp. salt
- ½ tsp. dried rosemary
- 2 minced garlic cloves
- ¼ C. olive oil
- 2.5 pounds' turkey breast loin

Directions:

- Mix pepper, salt, rosemary, garlic, and olive oil together. Spread herb mixture over turkey breast. Cover and chill 2 hours or overnight to marinade.
- Make sure to remove from fridge about half an hour before cooking.
- Ensure your air fryer is greased well and preheated to 400 degrees. Place loin into the fryer and cook 20 minutes
- Open fryer and spoon on butter mixture over turkey. Cook another 10 minutes
- Remove turkey from the fryer and let rest 5-10 minutes before attempting to slice.
- Slice against the grain and enjoy!

Nutrition: Calories 278 Fat 15g Protein 29g Carbs: 7g

4.28 Mexican Chicken Burgers

Preparation Time: 5 minutes

Cooking Time: 20 minutes

Total Time: 25 minutes **Servings:** 8

Ingredients:

- 1 jalapeno pepper
- 1 tsp. cayenne pepper
- 1 tbsp mustard powder
- 1 tbsp oregano
- 1 tbsp thyme
- 3 tbsp smoked paprika
- 1 beaten egg
- 1 small head of cauliflower
- 4 chicken breasts

Directions:

- Ensure your air fryer is preheated to 350 degrees.
- Add seasonings to a blender. Slice cauliflower into florets and add to blender.
- Pulse till mixture resembles that of breadcrumbs.
- Take out ¾ of cauliflower mixture and add to a bowl. Set to the side. In another bowl, beat your egg and set to the side.
- Remove skin and bones from chicken breasts and add to blender with remaining cauliflower mixture. Season it with pepper and salt.
- Take out mixture and form into burger shapes. Roll each patty in cauliflower crumbs, then the egg and back into crumbs again. Place coated patties into the air fryer, cooking 20 minutes
- Flip over at 10-minute mark. They are done when crispy!

Nutrition: Calories 234 Fat 18g Protein 24g Carbs: 1g

Nutritional Facts: Cal: 235 Carbs: 1.3 g Protein: 38 g Fat: 12 g

4.29 Taylor's Turkey Drumsticks

Servings: 6; **Preparation Time:** 5 mins

Cooking Time: 4 mins; **Total Time:** 9 mins

Ingredients:

- 6 turkey drumsticks
- 1 tbsp. of salt
- ½ of a cup of soy sauce
- 1 tsp. of ground black pepper
- ½ tsp. of garlic powder

Directions:

- Combine the pepper, salt and garlic powder in a small bowl and blend well.
- Rub the drumsticks all over generously with the mix.
- Into the Air fryer, pour in ½ of a cup of water and all the soy sauce and place the seasoned drumsticks inside.
- Close the lid and seal the valve.
- Set the pressure to high and cook for about 20 mins.
- After that time, allow the pressure to lower on its own for 13-16 mins and release the residual pressure quickly.
- Open the lid carefully and remove the drumsticks from the pot with tongs.
- Pour out the liquid and let it set for a bit.
- Skim the fat that will rise to the top and serve the juices alongside the drumsticks as a dipping sauce.

Nutritional Facts: Cal: 249 Fat: 1.2 g Carbs: 2.1 g Protein: 58 g

4.30 Bacon Chicken

Servings: 3; **Preparation Time**: 5 mins

Cooking Time: 15 mins; **Total Time**: 20 mins

Ingredients:

- 1 Breast of chicken
- 6 strips Unsmoked bacon
- 1 tbsp. soft garlic cheese

Directions:

- Slice the chicken into six portions.
- Spread the garlic cheese over each bacon strip.
- Add a piece of chicken to each one. Roll and secure with a toothpick.
- Prepare the Air Fryer ahead of fry time for about three mins.
- Arrange the wraps in the fryer basket. Air-fry them for about 15 mins.

Nutritional Facts: Cal: 4131.43 Protein: 325.44 g Carbs: 8.4 g Fat: 11/2 g

4.31 BBQ Chicken

Servings: 4; **Preparation Time**: 6 mins

Cooking Time: 14 mins; **Total Time**: 20 mins

Ingredients:

- 2 large Boneless - skinless chicken breast
- 1/2 cup Seasoned flour/Gluten-free seasoned flour
- 1 cup Barbecue sauce
- Olive oil cooking spray

Directions:

- Heat the Air Fryer to reach 390° Fahrenheit.
- Chop the chicken into bite-size chunks and place it in a mixing bowl.
- Coat the chunks with the experienced flour.

- Lightly spritz the basket of the Air Fryer with olive oil cooking spray and evenly pour the chicken into the cooker.
- Set the timer for 8 mins.
- Open the Air Fryer, coat the basket with olive oil spray, and flip the chicken as needed.
- Air-fry the chicken for eight more mins. Be sure its internal reading is at least 165° Fahrenheit.
- Place the chicken into a dish and add the sauce.
- Line the Air Fryer with a sheet of foil or add the chicken back to the fryer and cook for another 3 mins until the sauce is warmed and the chicken is a bit crispier and more coated.
- Serve.

Nutritional Facts: Cal. 615 Fat: 25.2 g Carbs: 3.3 g Protein: 89.6 g

4.32 Buffalo Wings

Servings: 2-3; **Preparation Time**: 10 mins

Cooking Time: 15 mins; **Total Time**: 25 mins

Ingredients:

- 1 tbsp. Butter - melted
- 5 /14 oz. Chicken wings
- 2 tsp. or to taste Cayenne pepper
- 2 tbsp. Red hot sauce
- 1/2 tsp. Optional: Garlic powder

Directions:

- Heat the Air Fryer temperature to reach 356° Fahrenheit.
- Slice the wings into three sections end tip, middle joint, and drumstick.
- Pat each one thoroughly dry using a paper towel.
- Combine the pepper, salt, garlic powder,

and cayenne pepper on a platter.

- Lightly cover the wings with the powder.
- Arrange the chicken onto the wire rack and bake for 15 mins, turning once at 7 mins.
- Combine the hot sauce with the melted butter in a dish to garnish the baked chicken when it is time to be served.

Nutritional Facts: Cal: 125 Fat: 1.2 g Carbs: 0.1 g Protein: 27 g

4.33 Chicken Chops

Servings: 4; **Preparation Time**: 10 mins

Cooking Time: 15 mins; **Total Time**: 25 mins

Ingredients:

- 2 tbsp. Butter/vegetable oil
- 3 tbsp. Breadcrumbs
- 1 Egg
- 8 Chicken tenderloins

Directions:

- Heat the Air Fryer temperature to 356° Fahrenheit.
- Combine the breadcrumbs and oil - stirring until the mixture crumbles.
- Whisk the egg and dredge the chicken through the egg, shaking off the excess.
- Dip each piece of chicken into the crumbs and evenly coat.
- Set the timer for 12 mins.

4.34 Chicken Strips

Servings: 4; **Preparation Time**: 10 mins

Cooking Time: 15 mins; **Total Time**: 25 mins

Ingredients:

- Chicken fillets 1 lb.
- Paprika 1 tsp.
- Heavy cream 1 tbsp.

- Black pepper 1/2 tsp.
- Butter as needed

Directions:

- Heat the Air Fryer at 365° Fahrenheit.
- Slice the fillets into strips and dust with salt and pepper.
- Add a light coating of butter to the basket.
- Arrange the strips in the basket and air-fry for six mins.
- Flip the strips and continue frying for another five mins.
- When done, garnish with the cream and paprika. Serve warm.

Nutritional Fact: Cal: 117.1 Fat: 6.4 g Carbs: 8.9 g Protein: 15 g

4.35 Eastern Chicken

Servings: 2; **Preparation Time**: 10 mins

Cooking Time: 30 mins; **Total Time**: 40 mins

Ingredients:

- 4 Chicken wings
- 1 tbsp. Chinese spice
- 1 tbsp. Mixed spices - your choice
- 1 tbsp. Soy sauce

Directions:

- Warm the Air Fryer to 356° Fahrenheit.
- Add the seasonings into a large mixing bowl, stirring thoroughly.
- Pour it over the chicken wings until each piece is covered.
- Put some aluminum foil on the base of the fryer and add the chicken sprinkling any remnants over the chicken. Air-fry it for 15 mins.
- Flip the chicken and air-fry for another 15 mins at 392° Fahrenheit.

Nutritional Facts: Cal: 590 Fat: 32 g Carbs: 9 g Protein: 69 g

4.36 Chicken Tenders

Servings: 4; **Preparation Time**: 5 mins

Cooking Time: 10 mins; **Total Time**: 15 mins

Ingredients:

- 3 Eggs
- 1 lb. Chicken tenders
- 1 cup Cornstarch
- 2 cups Sweetened shredded coconut
- 1 tsp. Cayenne pepper

Directions:

- Set the Air Fryer temperature at 360º Fahrenheit.
- Prepare three dishes. In the first one, add the cornstarch and cayenne with any other desired seasonings.
- In the second bowl, add the eggs.
- Lastly, add the coconut in the third dish.
- Dredge the chicken through the cornstarch, egg, and coconut.
- Lightly spritz the fryer basket with a cooking oil spray as needed. 10.
- Set the timer for 8 mins and air-fry until its golden brown before serving.

Nutritional Facts: Cal: 240 Protein: 13.9g Carbs: 2.7g Fat: 19.4g

4.37 Sliders

Servings: 6 = 12 sliders; **Prep Time**: 5 mins

Cooking Time: 10 mins; **Total Time**: 15 mins

Ingredients:

- 1 pkg. Tyson Crispy Chicken Strips
- 1 pkg. Sweet Hawaiian Rolls
- Optional Ingredients:
- Spinach leaves
- Tomatoes
- Honey mustard

Directions:

- Place the six chicken strips in the Air Fryer basket with a coating of olive oil spray.
- Cook at 390º Fahrenheit for 8 mins.
- Slice the rolls in half and top them with honey mustard, spinach, and tomatoes or other toppings of your choice.
- Slice the chicken strips into chunks and place them on the rolls.

Nutritional Facts: Cal. 615 Fat: 25.2 g Carbs: 3.3 g Protein: 89.6 g

4.38 Turkey Joint

Servings: 6; **Preparation Time**: 10 mins

Cooking Time: 50 minus; **Total Time**: 60 mins

Ingredients:

- 2 lb. Turkey breast
- 4 tbsp. Melted butter
- 3 cloves Garlic
- 1 tsp. Thyme
- 1 tsp. Rosemary

Directions:

- Warm the Air Fryer to reach 375° Fahrenheit.
- Pat the turkey breast dry.
- Mince the garlic and chop the rosemary and thyme.
- Melt the butter and mix with the garlic, thyme, and rosemary in a small mixing bowl.
- Brush the butter over turkey breast.
- Place in the Air Fryer basket, skin side up, and cook for 40 mins or until internal temperature reaches 160° Fahrenheit, flipping halfway through.
- Wait for five mins before slicing.

Nutritional Facts: Cal: 249 Fat: 1.2 g Carbs: 2.1 g Protein: 58 g

4.39 Honey Chicken Wings

Servings: 4; **Prepa Time**: 10 mins

Cooking Time: 30 mins; **Total Time**: 40 mins

Ingredients:

- 2 lb. Chicken wings
- 2 tbsp. Lime juice
- 1/4 cup Honey
- 1 tbsp. Lime zest
- 1 pressed Garlic clove

Directions:

- Warm the Air Fryer at 360° Fahrenheit.
- Whisk the garlic, honey, and lime juice and zest.
- Toss in the wings and cover with the mixture.
- Prepare the wings in batches.
- Cook for 25-30 mins until they're crispy.
- Shake the basket at 8-minute intervals.
- Serve and garnish as desired.

Nutritional Facts: Cal: 249 Fat: 1.2 g Carbs: 2.1 g Protein: 58 g

4.40 Rotisserie Chicken

Servings: 4; **Preparation Time**: 20 mins

Cooking Time: 60 mins; **Total Time**: 90 mins

Ingredients:

- 2 tsp. Olive oil or as needed
- 6-7 lb. Whole chicken
- 1 tbsp. Seasoned salt

Directions:

- Set the Air Fryer at 350° Fahrenheit.
- Coat the chicken with oil and a sprinkle of salt.
- Arrange the chicken in the Air Fryer – skin-side down.
- Cook for 30 mins. Flip the chicken over and air- fry for another 30 mins.
- Wait for ten mins before slicing
- Note: This recipe is for chickens under 6 lb. for a 3.7-quart Air Fryer.

Nutritional Facts: Cal: 590 Fat: 32 g Carbs: 9 g Protein: 69 g

4.41 Crispy Southern Fried Chicken

Preparation Time: 10 minutes

Cooking Time: 25 minutes

Total Time: 35 minutes

Servings: 4

Ingredients:

- 1 tsp. cayenne pepper
- 2 tbsp mustard powder
- 2 tbsp oregano
- 2 tbsp thyme
- 3 tbsp coconut milk
- 1 beaten egg
- ¼ C. cauliflower
- ¼ C. gluten-free oats
- 8 chicken drumsticks

Directions:

- Ensure air fryer is preheated to 350 degrees.
- Lay out chicken and Season it with pepper and salt on all sides.
- Add all other ingredients to a blender, blending till a smooth-like breadcrumb mixture is created. Place in a bowl and add a beaten egg to another bowl.
- Dip chicken into breadcrumbs, then into egg and breadcrumbs once more.
- Place coated drumsticks into air fryer and cook 20 minutes Bump up the temperature to 390 degrees and cook another 5 minutes till crispy..

Nutrition: Calories 504 Fat 18g Protein 35g Carbs: 5g

4.42 California Chicken

Servings: 6/8 servings; **Prep Time:** 2 mins

Cooking Time: 8 mins; **Total Time:** 10 mins

Ingredients:

- 4 pounds of skinless, boneless chicken breast
- ½ of a tsp. of sea salt
- ½ of a tsp. of ground black pepper
- 1 tbsp. of Italian seasoning pre-mixed
- 1 cup of chicken broth

Directions:

- Season the chicken breasts generously on both sides with sea salt, pepper, and Italian seasoning.
- You can also use other spices and herbs of your choice.
- Place the breasts inside the Air fryer and carefully pour in the broth.
- Pour around the meat as to not wash off the seasonings.
- Secure the lid and choose the Poultry setting or Manual on the control panel.
- For breasts that are about 6-8 ounces, the cooking time is 8 mins for fresh and 13 mins for frozen meat.
- If your chicken breasts are smaller or larger than that, tweak the time as needed.
- After the time is up, let the pressure release on its own – this will yield the tenderest meat.
- If you are pressed for time, allow the natural release for 5-7 mins and then release the rest quickly.
- You can now unplug the air fryer and start shredding the chicken. Work with two forks.
- You can take the breasts out but shredding them inside the pot will make them juicier as they mix with the broth.
- If you want to serve the chicken immediately, allow it to drain for a bit, but in can be stored in the broth for later – it will help it stay moist.

Nutritional Facts: Cal: 249 Fat: 1.2 g Carbs: 2.1 g Protein: 58

4.43 Chicken Kabobs

Preparation Time: 15 minutes

Cooking Time: 20 minutes

Total Time: 35 minutes **Servings:** 4

Ingredients:

- 2 diced chicken breasts
- 3 bell peppers
- 6 mushrooms
- Sesame seeds
- 1/3 C. low-Sodium soy sauce
- 1/3 C. raw honey

Directions:

- Chop up chicken into cubes, seasoning with a few sprays of olive oil, pepper, and salt.
- Dice up bell peppers and cut mushrooms in half. Mix soy sauce and honey together till well combined. Add sesame seeds and stir.
- Skewer chicken, peppers, and mushrooms onto wooden skewers. Ensure air fryer is pre-heated to 388 degrees. Coat the kabobs with honey-soy sauce.
- Place coated kabobs in air fryer basket and cook 15-20 minutes

Nutrition: Calories 296 Fat 13g Protein 17g Carbs: 1g

4.44 Mustard Chicken Tenders

Preparation Time: 10 minutes

Cooking Time: 15 minutes

Total Time: 25 minutes

Servings: 6

Ingredients:

- ½ C. coconut flour
- 1 tbsp spicy brown mustard
- 2 beaten eggs
- 1 pound of chicken tenders

Directions:

- Season tenders with pepper and salt.
- Place a thin layer of mustard onto tenders and then dredge in flour and dip in egg.
- Add to air fryer and cook 10-15 minutes at 390 degrees till crispy.

Nutrition: Calories 403 Fat 20g Protein 22g Carbs: 4g

CHAPTER 5:
Vegetables Recipes

The selection of recipes below carefully considered to introduce you to the Mediterranean diet through air-fried foods. You will experience flavors that are common and some that will take you on a journey to the Mediterranean Sea. Get ready to be blown away by the skillful use of healthy ingredients that will satisfy your savory and sweet cravings while offering you a lot of nutritional value too! Are you trying to go down a dress size? These delicious recipes will allow you to lose weight, improve your overall well-being, and boost your body's natural energy without having to restrict any foods. At the end of the day, it's all about consuming foods in moderation, and enjoying life in between!

5.1 Parmesan Hasselback Potatoes

Serving: 4/5; **Preparation Time**: 10 mins

Cooking Time: 25 mins; **Total Time**: 35 mins

Ingredients:

- 1½ pounds (680 g) baby Yukon Gold potatoes
- 5 tbsp. cashew butter
- Salt and freshly ground black pepper
- 1 tbsp. vegetable oil
- ¼ cup grated Parmesan cheese (optional) Chopped fresh parsley or chives

Directions:

- Preheat the air fryer to 400°F (204°C).
- Make six to eight deep vertical slits across the top of each potato about three quarters of the way down.
- Make sure the slits are deep enough to allow the slices to spread apart a little, but don't cut all the way through the potato.
- Place a thin layer of butter between each of the slices and season generously with salt and pepper.
- Transfer the potatoes to the air fryer basket.
- Pack them in next to each other. It's alright if some of the potatoes sit on top or

rest on another potato. Air fry for 20 mins.
- Spray or brush the potatoes with a little vegetable oil and sprinkle the Parmesan cheese on top (if using). Air fry for an additional 5 mins.
- Garnish with chopped parsley or chives and serve hot.

Nutritional Facts: Cal: 590 Fat: 32 g Carbs: 9 g Protein: 69 g

5.2 Lemon Potatoes with Rosemary

Serving: 4; **Preparation Time**: 10 mins

Cooking Time: 25 mins; **Total Time**: 35 mins

Ingredients:

- 1 pound (454 g) small, red-skinned potatoes, halved or cut into bite-sized chunks
- 1 tbsp. olive oil
- 1 tsp. finely chopped fresh rosemary
- ¼ tsp. salt
- Freshly ground black pepper
- 1 tbsp. lemon zest

Directions:

- Preheat the air fryer to 400°F (204°C).
- Toss the potatoes with the olive oil, rosemary, salt and freshly ground black pepper.
- Air fry for 12 mins (depending on the size of the chunks), tossing the potatoes a few times throughout the cooking process.
- As soon as the potatoes are tender to a knifepoint, toss them with the lemon zest and more salt if desired.

Nutritional Facts: Cal: 220 Fat: 12 g Carbs: 45 g Protein: 80 g

5.3 Parsley Shiitake Mushrooms

Serving: 4; **Preparation Time:** 10 mins

Cooking Time: 25 mins; **Total Time:** 55 mins

Ingredients:

- 8 ounces (227 g) shiitake mushrooms, stems removed, and caps roughly chopped
- 1 tbsp. olive oil
- ½ tsp. salt
- Freshly ground black pepper
- 1 tsp. chopped fresh thyme leaves
- 1 tsp. chopped fresh oregano
- 1 tbsp. chopped fresh parsley

Directions:

- Preheat the air fryer to 400°F (204°C).
- Toss the mushrooms with the olive oil, salt, pepper, thyme, and oregano.
- Air fry for 5 mins, shaking the basket once or twice during the cooking process.
- The mushrooms will still be somewhat chewy with a meaty texture.
- If you'd like them a little more tender, add a couple of mins to this cooking time.
- Once cooked, add the parsley to the mushrooms and toss.
- Season again to taste and serve.

Nutritional Facts: Cal: 200 Fat: 22 g Carbs: 60 g Protein: 80 g

5.4 Ratatouille Vegetables with Basil

Serving: 2/4; **Preparation Time:** 15 mins

Cooking Time: 15mins; **Total Time:** 30 mins

Ingredients:

- 1 baby or Japanese eggplant, cut into 1½-inch cubes
- 1 red pepper, cut into 1-inch chunks
- 1 yellow pepper, cut into 1-inch chunks
- 1 zucchini, cut into 1-inch chunks
- 1 clove garlic, minced
- ½ tsp. dried basil
- 1 tbsp. olive oil
- Salt and freshly ground black pepper
- ¼ cup sliced sun-dried tomatoes in oil
- 2 tbsp. chopped fresh basil

Directions:

- Preheat the air fryer to 400°F (204°C).
- Toss the eggplant, peppers and zucchini with the garlic, dried basil, olive oil, salt and freshly ground black pepper.
- Air fries the vegetables at 400°F (204°C) for 15 mins, shaking the basket a few times during the cooking process to redistribute the ingredients.
- As soon as the vegetables are tender, toss them with the sliced sun- dried tomatoes and fresh basil and serve.

Nutritional Facts: Cal: 300 Fat: 22 g Carbs: 89 g Protein: 100 g

5.5 Sugar Snap Peas and Carrots with Sesame

Serving: 4; **Preparation Time:** 6 mins

Cooking Time: 15 mins; **Total Time**: 21 mins

Ingredients:

- 1-pound (454 g) carrots, peeled sliced on the bias (½-inch slices)
- 1 tsp. olive oil
- Salt and freshly ground black pepper
- ⅓ cup honey
- 1 tbsp. sesame oil
- 1 tbsp. soy sauce
- ½ tsp. minced fresh ginger
- 4 ounces (113 g) sugar snap peas
- 1½ tsp. sesame seeds

Directions:

- Preheat the air fryer to 360°F (182°C).
- Toss the carrots with the olive oil, season with salt and pepper and air fry for 10 mins, shaking the basket once or twice during the cooking process.
- Combine the honey, sesame oil, soy sauce and minced ginger in a large bowl.
- Add the sugar snap peas and the air-fried carrots to the honey mixture, toss to coat and return everything to the air fryer basket.
- Turn up the temperature to 400°F (204°C) and air fry for an additional 6 mins, shaking the basket once during the cooking process.
- Transfer the carrots and sugar snap peas to a serving bowl.
- Pour the sauce from the bottom of the cooker over the vegetables and sprinkle sesame seeds over top.
- Serve immediately.

Nutritional Facts: Cal: 230 Fat: 20 g Carbs: 97 g Protein: 65 g

5.6 Balsamic Pearl Onions with Basil

Serving: 2 to 4; **Preparation Time**: 5 mins

Cooking Time: 10 mins; **Total Time**: 15 mins

Ingredients:

- 1 pound (454 g) fresh pearl onions
- 1 tbsp. olive oil
- Salt and freshly ground black pepper
- 1 tsp. high quality aged balsamic vinegar
- 1 tbsp. chopped fresh basil leaves (or mint)

Directions:

- Preheat the air fryer to 400°F (204°C).
- Decide whether you want to peel the onions before or after they cook.
- Peeling them ahead of time is a little more laborious.
- Peeling after they cook is easier, but a little messier since the onions are hot and you may discard more of the onion than you'd like to.
- If you opt to peel them first, trim the tiny root of the onions off and pinch off any loose papery skins. (It's ok if there are some skins left on the onions.) Toss the pearl onions with the olive oil, salt and freshly ground black pepper.
- Air fry for 10 mins, shaking the basket a couple of times during the cooking process. (If your pearl onions are very large, you may need to add a couple of mins to this cooking time.)
- Let the onions cool slightly and then slip off any remaining skins.
- Toss the onions with the balsamic vinegar and basil and serve.

Nutritional Facts: Cal: 150 Fat: 15 g Carbs: 88 g Protein: 44

5.7 Cardamom-Orange Carrots with Chives

Serving: 4; **Preparation Time**: 15 mins

Cooking Time: 30 mins; **Total Time**: 45 mins

Ingredients:

- 2 tbsp. cashew butter
- 1 tbsp. honey
- ½ tsp. grated orange zest plus
- 1 tbsp. juice
- ½ tsp. ground cardamom
- Salt and pepper
- 2 pounds (907 g) carrots, peeled and cut into 2-inch lengths, thick ends halved lengthwise
- 1 tbsp. minced fresh chives

Directions:

- Microwave butter, honey, orange zest, cardamom, and ¼ tsp. salt in large bowl at 50 percent power, stirring occasionally, about 1 minute.
- Whisk to combine. Combine 1 tbsp. butter mixture and orange juice in small bowl; set aside.
- Add carrots to remaining butter mixture and toss to coat; transfer to air fryer basket.
- Place basket in air fryer and set temperature to 400°F (204°C).
- Cook carrots until tender and browned, about 30 mins, tossing every 10 mins.
- Transfer carrots to now-empty bowl and toss with reserved butter mixture.
- Season with salt and pepper to taste and sprinkle with chives.
- Serve.

Nutritional Facts: Cal: 490 Fat: 28 g Carbs: 87 g Protein: 55 g

5.8 Chickpea and Curried Cauliflower Salad

Serving: 4; **Preparation Time**: 20 mins

Cooking Time: 23 mins; **Total Time**: 43 mins

Ingredients:

- 3½ tbsp. extra-virgin olive oil
- 1½ tsp. curry powder
- Salt and pepper
- 1 head cauliflower, cored and cut into 1½-inch florets
- ¼ cup plain Greek yogurt
- 2 tbsp. chopped fresh cilantro
- 1½ tsp. lime juice
- 1 garlic clove, minced
- 1 (15-ounce / 425-g) can chickpeas, rinsed
- 3 ounces (85 g) seedless red grapes, halved
- ¼ cup roasted cashews, chopped

Directions:

- Whisk 1½ tbsp. oil, curry powder, ⅛ tsp. salt, and ⅛ tsp. pepper together in medium bowl.
- Add cauliflower and toss to coat, transfer to air fryer basket.
- Place basket in air fryer and set temperature to 400°F (204°C).
- Cook cauliflower until tender and golden at edges, 23 to 25 mins, tossing halfway through cooking. Set cauliflower aside to cool slightly.
- Meanwhile, whisk yogurt, 1 tbsp. cilantro, lime juice, garlic, ⅛ tsp. salt, ⅛ tsp. pepper, and remaining 2 tbsp. oil together in serving bowl.
- Add cooled cauliflower and chickpeas and toss to coat.
- Season with salt and pepper to taste.
- Sprinkle with grapes, cashews, and remaining 1 tbsp. cilantro and Serve.

Nutritional Facts: Cal: 440 Fat: 12 g Carbs: 50 g Protein: 39 g

5.9 Green Beans with Sun-Dried Tomatoes

Serving: 4; **Preparation Time**: 12 mins

Cooking Time: 15 mins; **Total Time**: 17 mins

Ingredients:

- 1 pound (454 g) green beans, trimmed and halved
- 2 tsp. extra-virgin olive oil
- Salt and pepper
- ½ cup torn fresh basil
- ⅓ cup oil-packed sun-dried tomatoes, rinsed, patted dry, and chopped
- 1 tbsp. lemon juice
- 2 ounces (57 g) goat cheese, crumbled
- ¼ cup roasted sunflower seeds

Directions:

- Toss green beans with 1 tsp. oil, ⅛ tsp. salt, and ⅛ tsp. pepper in bowl: transfer to air fryer basket.
- Place basket in air fryer and set temperature to 400°F (204°C).
- Cook green beans until crisp-tender, 12 to 15 mins, tossing halfway through cooking.
- Toss green beans with remaining 1 tsp. oil, basil, sun-dried tomatoes, and lemon juice in large bowl.
- Season with salt and pepper to taste.
- Transfer to serving dish and sprinkle with goat cheese and sunflower seeds.
- Serve.

Nutritional Facts: Cal: 390 Fat: 22 g Carbs: 72 g Protein: 77 g

5.10 Sage Butternut Squash with Hazelnuts

Serving: 4; **Preparation Time**: 15 mins

Cooking Time: 30 mins; **Total Time**: 45 mins

Ingredients:

- 2 tbsp. cashew butter
- tbsp. minced fresh sage
- 1 tsp. lemon juice
- Salt and pepper
- 5 pounds (907 g) butternut squash, peeled, seeded, and cut into 1-inch pieces
- ⅓ cup skinned raw hazelnuts, chopped coarse

Directions:

- Microwave butter and sage in large bowl at 50 percent power, stirring occasionally, about 1 minute.
- Transfer 1 tbsp. butter mixture to small bowl, then stir in lemon juice and ⅛ tsp. salt; set aside.
- Add squash, ¼ tsp. salt, and ⅛ tsp. pepper to remaining butter mixture and toss to coat.
- Place squash in air fryer basket.
- Place basket in air fryer, set temperature to 400°F (204°C), and cook for 15 mins.
- Stir in hazelnuts and cook until squash is tender and well browned, 15 to 20 mins, tossing halfway through cooking.
- Transfer squash mixture to clean large bowl; toss with reserved butter mixture.
- Season with salt and pepper to taste.
- Serve.

Nutritional Facts: Cal: 560 Fat: 10 g Carbs: 55 g Protein: 100g

5.11 Cheese Zucchini Rice Fritters

Serving: 4; **Preparation Time**: 15 mins

Cooking Time: 12 mins; **Total Time**: 27 mins

Ingredients:

- 2 cups (495 g) cooked rice
- 2 cups grated cheese, such as Cheddar, Swiss, or Gruyère
- 1 medium zucchini, grated
- 4 scallions, white and light green parts only, sliced
- ¼ cup tightly packed chopped fresh mint
- 3 eggs, beaten
- Kosher salt and pepper to taste
- 1¼ cups whole wheat breadcrumbs
- Vegetable oil for spraying
- Lemon wedges for serving

Directions:

- Combine the cooked rice, grated cheese, grated zucchini, scallions, and mint in a large bowl.
- Add the beaten eggs and season with salt and pepper.
- Stir to combine, making sure the egg is evenly distributed through the rice.
- Spread the breadcrumbs on a plate.
- Scoop out approximately ½ cup (82½ g) of the rice mixture and form into a ball with your hands, pressing firmly to make the fritters as tight and well-packed as possible.
- Dredge the ball in the breadcrumbs.
- Repeat with the remaining rice mixture.
- You should be able to make 8 or 9 fritters.
- Place half the fritters on a plate and chill until needed.
- Spray the remaining half of the rice fritters and the basket of the air fryer with oil to prevent sticking.
- Place the fritters in the basket of the air fryer and cook at 400°F (204°C) until

browned on all sides and cooked through, 10 to 12 mins.

- Carefully remove the fritters to a platter and place the remaining fritters in the air fryer and cook in the same manner.
- Serve the rice fritters with lemon wedges for spritzing.

Nutritional Facts: Cal: 300 Fat: 22 g Carbs: 89 g Protein: 100 g

5.12 Scallion Tofu

Serving: 4; **Preparation Time**: 10 mins

Cooking Time: 14 mins; **Total Time**: 24 mins

Ingredients:

- 14 ounces (397 g) extra-firm tofu, preferably silken
- ¼ cup plus
- 2 tbsp. cornstarch
- 1½ tsp. fine sea salt
- 2 tsp. freshly ground black pepper
- Vegetable oil for spraying
- scallions, white and green parts only, sliced

Directions:

- Place the tofu on a paper towel-lined plate.
- Cover with another plate and place something heavy, such as a can from your pantry, on top of the plate.
- Press the tofu in this manner for 20 mins to remove some of the liquid.
- When the tofu has drained, cut it into 1-inch (2½ cm) cubes. Place the cornstarch, salt, and pepper in a medium bowl.
- Place the tofu cubes in the bowl and toss them in the cornstarch mixture until they are coated on all sides.
- Remove half of the tofu cubes from the

bowl, leaving the other half in the cornstarch, and shake each one to remove any excess cornstarch.

- Place the coated tofu cubes on a plate.
- Spray the basket of the air fryer with oil.
- Arrange half of the tofu cubes in a single layer in the basket, taking care not to crowd them. Spray the cubes well with oil.
- Cook at 400°F (204°C) for 12 to 14 mins, shaking the basket once or twice during cooking to toss the cubes.
- If you notice cornstarch on the outside of the cubes that is not browning, spray those areas with additional oil.
- When the first batch of tofu cubes is light golden in color on all sides and there are no visible patches of cornstarch remaining, remove to a plate.
- Remove the second batch of tofu cubes from the cornstarch and cook in the same manner.
- Serve warm garnished with scallions. (The tofu will lose the crispy texture as it cools.)

Nutritional Facts: Cal: 220 Fat: 12 g Carbs: 45 g Protein: 80 g

5.13 Masala-Glazed Potato Chips

Serving: 2; **Preparation Time**: 20 mins

Cooking Time: 36 mins; **Total Time**: 56 mins

Ingredients:

- 2 large russet potatoes
- 3 tbsp. olive oil 3 cloves garlic, minced
- 1-piece fresh ginger, peeled and grated
- ½ yellow onion, diced
- 2 tsp. kosher salt, divided
- 1 serrano pepper, seeded and minced
- 1½ tsp. garam masala
- ½ tsp. cumin
- ¼ tsp. turmeric
- tbsp. tomato pastes 2 medium tomatoes, diced
- 2 tsp. vegetable oil Juice of
- 1 lemon
- 2 tbsp. chopped cilantro
- 2 tbsp. crumbly hard cheese such as a mild feta, paneer, or queso fresco

Directions:

- Peel the potatoes and cut them into ¼-inch (6 mm) slices.
- Cut each slice into 4 or 5 thick fries. (Halve any especially long pieces.
- You're looking for fries the size of your finger.)
- Place the cut potatoes into a bowl of cold water and let them soak for at least 30 mins to get rid of excess starch.
- While the potatoes are soaking, make the masala.
- Heat the oil in a large, deep skillet over medium heat.
- Add the garlic and ginger and cook for 1 minute, stirring.
- Add the onion and season with 1 tsp. of the salt.
- Sauté the onion, stirring, for 5 mins.
- Add the serrano pepper and spices and

saúté for 3 additional mins.

- Add the tomato paste and diced tomatoes to the skillet and stir to combine.
- Sauté the tomatoes until they begin to break down and form a sauce, about 5 mins.
- Remove the skillet from the heat and set aside.
- Preheat the air fryer to 400°F (204°C). Drain the potatoes and dry them well.
- Toss the potatoes with the oil and remaining tsp. of salt.
- Arrange the potatoes in a single layer in the basket of the air fryer. (Depending on the size of your machine, you may have to work in 2 batches.
- Do not overcrowd the basket.) Cook for 10 mins.
- Open the air fryer and shake the basket to redistribute the potatoes.
- Cook for an additional 10 to 12 mins until all the potatoes are browned and crisp.
- Place the fries in the skillet with the masala sauce and add the lemon juice. Toss to coat with the sauce and cook over medium heat for a few mins until warmed through.
- Arrange the masala fries on a platter and garnish with chopped cilantro and crumbled cheese. Serve immediately.

Nutritional Facts: Cal: 200 Fat: 22 g Carbs: 60 g Protein: 80 g

5.14 Cauliflower Steaks with Tahini-Lemon Sauce

Serving: 3 to 4; **Preparation Time**: 20 mins

Cooking Time: 17 mins; **Total Time**: 57 mins

Ingredients:

- Tahini Sauce:
- ½ cup tahini
- ½ cup freshly squeezed lemon juice
- 2 tbsp. extra-virgin olive oil
- ½ cup warm water
- Cauliflower Steaks:
- 2 heads cauliflower
- 1 cup whole wheat flour
- 2 cups whole wheat breadcrumbs
- 2 tsp. thyme
- 2 tsp. oregano
- 1 tsp. kosher salt
- 1 tsp. black pepper
- 2 eggs beaten with
- 2 tbsp. water Vegetable oil for spraying
- ¼ cup chopped flat-leaf parsley
- Lemon wedges for serving

Directions:

- To make the tahini sauce, combine the tahini, lemon juice, and olive oil in a small bowl.
- Slowly whisk in the water until you reach the desired consistency, (You may not need the entire ½ cup.) Set aside.
- To make the cauliflower steaks, remove the leaves and trim the stems of the cauliflower, leaving the cores intact.
- Stand the cauliflower on a cutting board.
- Using a large knife, slice off the rounded sides of the cauliflower, leaving the middle section still attached to the core.
- Slice this middle section into 2 or 3 flat "steaks," depending on the size of the

cauliflower, 1 to 1½ inches (21/2 to 4 cm) thick.

- Place the flour in a shallow dish or pie plate.
- In a separate shallow dish, combine the breadcrumbs, thyme, oregano, salt, and pepper.
- Dredge 2 of the cauliflower steaks first in the flour, then the egg mixture, and finally the panko mixture, coating both sides.
- Remove to a plate.
- Preheat the air fryer to 375°F (191°C).
- Spray both sides of the cauliflower steaks with oil and place in the basket of the air fryer.
- Cook for 15 to 17 mins, flipping the steaks once halfway through, until the cauliflower is fork-tender, and the breading is browned and crispy.
- Repeat with the remaining steaks.
- Drizzle tahini sauce over the steaks and serve with parsley and lemon wedges.

Nutritional Facts: Cal: 220 Fat: 12 g Carbs: 45 g Protein: 80 g

5.15 Broccoli and Farro Bowls

Servings: 2 grain bowls; **Prepa Time**: 16 mins

Cooking Time: 20 mins; **Total Time**: 36 mins

Ingredients:

- Creamy Herb Dressing:
- ½ cup plain Greek yogurt
- ½ cup fresh cilantro or basil leaves
- 2 tbsp. extra-virgin olive oil
- 1 clove garlic, peeled
- Juice of 1 lemon
- ½ tsp. kosher salt
- ½ tsp. cumin
- Grain Bowls:
- 1 cup diced sweet potatoes

- 2 cups broccoli florets
- 1 tsp. kosher salt, divided
- 1 tsp. extra-virgin olive oil, divided
- 2 cups cooked and cooled pearled farro
- ½ small red onion, thinly sliced
- 1 small avocado, pitted and diced Kosher salt and pepper to taste

Directions:

- To make the Creamy Herb Dressing, combine all dressing ingredients in a blender.
- Blend on medium speed until completely combined and smooth.
- If the dressing is too thick, add 1 to 2 tbsp. of water.
- Combine the sweet potatoes, broccoli, and ½ tsp. of the salt in a bowl with 1 tsp. of the olive oil and toss to combine.
- Arrange the vegetables in a single layer in the basket of the air fryer and cook at 350°F (177°C) until the potatoes are golden brown and the broccoli is tender and starting to brown on the tops, about 8 mins.
- Transfer the vegetables to a platter and keep warm.

Nutritional Facts: Cal: 440 Fat: 12 g Carbs: 50 g Protein: 39 g

5.16 Patatas Bravas

Preparation time: 25 minutes
Cooking time: 20 minutes
Total Time: 45 minutes **Servings:** 4
Ingredients:

- 12 ounces red potato, cut into 1-inch chunks
- 1/2 teaspoon ground black pepper
- 1/2 teaspoon sea salt
- 1 teaspoon garlic powder
- 1/2 teaspoon cayenne pepper
- 1 tablespoon smoked paprika
- 1 tablespoon coconut oil
- ¼ teaspoon dried chives
- Garlic aioli for serving

Directions:

- Take a pot, place it half-full with water over medium heat, bring the water to boil, add potato pieces, and cook for 6 minutes.
- Then drain the potatoes, pat them dry, cool for 15 minutes and add them into a large bowl.
- Add garlic into the potatoes, season with 1/8 teaspoon each of salt and black pepper, drizzle with oil and toss until coated.
- Switch on the air fryer, insert fryer basket, grease it with olive oil, then shut with its lid, set the fryer at 390 degrees F, and preheat for 5 minutes.
- Open the fryer, add potatoes in it in a single layer, pour and stir a tablespoon of olive oil, close with its lid and cook for 15 minutes until nicely golden and crispy, shaking the basket halfway through.
- When air fryer beeps, open its lid, transfer potatoes to a bowl, add remaining ingredients, toss until coated, and serve them with garlic aioli.

Nutrition: Calories: 97 Fat: 4 g Carbs: 15 g Protein: 1 g

5.17 Broccoli and Carrot Medley

Serving: 4; **Preparation Time:** 5 mins

Cooking Time: 15 mins; **Total Time:** 20 mins

Ingredients:

- 1 head broccoli, chopped
- 2 medium carrots, cut into 1-inch pieces Salt
- Pepper
- Cooking oil
- 1 zucchini, cut into 1-inch chunks
- 1 medium red bell pepper, seeded and thinly sliced

Directions:

- In a large bowl, combine the broccoli and carrots.
- Season with salt and pepper to taste.
- Spray with cooking oil.
- Transfer the broccoli and carrots to the air fryer basket.
- Cook at 390°F (199°C) for 6 mins.
- Place the zucchini and red pepper in the bowl.
- Season with salt and pepper to taste.
- Spray with cooking oil.
- Add the zucchini and red pepper to the broccoli and carrots in the air fryer basket.
- Cook for 6 mins.
- Cool before serving.

Nutritional Facts: Cal: 150 Fat: 15 g Carbs: 88 g Protein: 44 g

5.18 Mozzarella Veggie-Stuffed Peppers

Serving: 4; **Preparation Time**: 15 mins

Cooking Time: 15 mins; **Total Time**: 30 mins

Ingredients:

- 4 large red bell peppers
- 1½ cups cooked rice
- ¼ cup chopped onion
- ¼ cup sliced mushrooms
- ¾ cup marinara sauce Salt
- Pepper
- ¾ cup shredded mozzarella cheese

Directions:

- Boil a large pot of water over high heat.
- Cut off the tops of the peppers.
- You can save the tops for decorative plating after you have cooked the peppers.
- Remove the seeds and hollow out the inside of the peppers.
- Add the peppers to the boiling water for 5 mins.
- Remove and allow them to cool for 3 to 4 mins.
- In a large bowl, combine the cooked rice, onion, mushrooms, and marinara sauce.
- Season with salt and pepper to taste.
- Stuff the peppers with the rice mixture.
- Sprinkle the mozzarella cheese on top of the peppers.
- Place the stuffed peppers in the air fryer. Cook at 350°F (177°C) for 10 mins.
- Cool before serving.

Nutritional Facts: Cal: 130 Fat: 20 g Carbs: 102 g Protein: 78 g

5.19 Air Fryer Corn on the Cob

Serving: 4; **Preparation Time**: 10 mins

Cooking Time: 10 mins; **Total Time**: 20 mins

Ingredients:

- 4 ears corn, shucked and halved crosswise
- 1 tbsp. extra-virgin olive oil
- Salt Pepper

Directions:

- Place the corn in a large bowl.
- Coat with the olive oil and season with salt and pepper to taste.
- Place the corn in the air fryer.
- Cook at 390°F (199°C) for 6 mins.
- Cool before serving.

Nutritional Facts: Cal: 220 Fat: 12 g Carbs: 45 g Protein: 80 g

5.20 Feta Veggie-Stuffed Portobellos

Serving: 4; **Preparation Time**: 12 mins

Cooking Time: 20 mins; **Total Time**: 32 mins

Ingredients:

- 4 large portobello mushroom caps (about 3 ounces / 85 g each) Olive oil spray
- Kosher salt
- ¼ cup of chopped fresh basil
- 2 tbsp. of whole wheat bread crumbs
- 2 medium plum tomatoes, chopped
- ¾ cup of feta cheese, crumbled
- 1 clove of garlic, minced
- 1 shallot, chopped
- 1 tbsp. of chopped fresh oregano
- 1 tbsp. of freshly grated Parmesan cheese
- ⅛ tsp. of freshly ground black pepper
- 1 cup of baby spinach, roughly chopped
- 1 tbsp. of olive oil
- Balsamic glaze (optional), for drizzling

Directions:

- Use a small metal spoon to carefully

scrape the black gills out of each mushroom cap.

- Spray both sides of the mushrooms with olive oil and season with a pinch of salt.
- In a medium bowl, combine the tomatoes, spinach, feta, shallot, garlic, basil, breadcrumbs, oregano, Parmesan, ¼ tsp. salt, pepper, and olive oil and mix well.
- Carefully fill the inside of each mushroom cap with the mixture.
- Preheat the air fryer to 370°F (188°C).
- Working in batches, arrange a single layer of the stuffed mushrooms in the air fryer basket.
- Cook for 10 to 12 mins, until the mushrooms are tender, and the top is golden.
- Use a flexible spatula to carefully remove the mushrooms from the basket and transfer to a serving dish.
- Drizzle the balsamic glaze (if using) over the mushrooms and serve.

Nutritional Facts: Cal: 440 Fat: 12 g Carbs: 50 g Protein: 39 g

5.21 Parmesan Zucchini Fries

Serving: 4; **Preparation Time**: 20 mins

Cooking Time: 20 mins; **Total Time**: 40 mins

Ingredients:

- 1 cup yellow cornmeal
- 1 tsp. Creole Seasoning
- 1 tsp. salt
- ½ tsp. freshly ground black pepper
- 2 large eggs, beaten
- ¼ cup grated Parmesan cheese
- 1½ cups whole wheat breadcrumbs
- 2 zucchinis, peeled and cut into 1-inch-thick strips
- 1 to 2 tbsp. oil

Directions:

- In a shallow dish, whisk the cornmeal, Creole Seasoning, salt, and pepper until blended.
- Place the beaten eggs in a second shallow bowl and stir together the Parmesan cheese and breadcrumbs in a third bowl.
- One at a time, dip the zucchini into the cornmeal, the beaten eggs, and the breadcrumbs, coating thoroughly.
- Preheat the air fryer to 350°F (177°C). Line the air fryer tray with parchment paper.
- Place half the zucchini fries on the parchment and spritz with oil.
- Cook for 4 mins.
- Shake the basket, spritz the fries with oil, and cook for 4 to 6 mins more until lightly browned and crispy.
- Repeat with the remaining fries.

Nutritional Facts: Cal: 200 Fat: 22 g Carbs: 60 g Protein: 80 g

5.22 Sriracha Green Bean and Tofu Fry

Serving: 4 to 6; **Preparation Time**: 25 mins

Cooking Time: 17 mins; **Total Time**: 42 mins

Ingredients:

- 4 tsp. canola oil, divided
- 2 tbsp. rice wine vinegar
- 1 tbsp. sriracha chili sauce
- ¼ cup soy sauce
- ½ tsp. toasted sesame oil
- 1 tsp. minced garlic
- 1 tbsp. minced fresh ginger
- 8 ounces (227 g) extra firm tofu
- ½ cup vegetable stock or water 1 tbsp. honey
- 1 tbsp. cornstarch
- ½ red onion, chopped
- 1 red or yellow bell pepper, chopped
- 1 cup green beans, cut into 2-inch lengths
- 4 ounces (113 g) mushrooms, sliced
- scallions, sliced
- 2 tbsp. fresh cilantro leaves
- 2 tsp. toasted sesame seeds

Directions:

- Combine 1 tbsp. of the oil, vinegar, sriracha sauce, soy sauce, sesame oil, garlic, and ginger in a small bowl.
- Cut the tofu into bite-sized cubes and toss the tofu in with the marinade while you prepare the other vegetables.
- When you are ready to start cooking, remove the tofu from the marinade and set it aside.
- Add the water, honey and cornstarch to the marinade and bring to a simmer on the stovetop, just until the sauce thickens.
- Set the sauce aside.

- Preheat the air fryer to 400ºF (204ºC).
- Toss the onion, pepper, green beans, and mushrooms in a bowl with a little canola oil and season with salt.
- Air fry at 400ºF (204ºC) for 10 to 12 mins, shaking the basket and tossing the vegetables every few mins.
- When the vegetables are cooked to your preferred doneness, remove them from the air fryer and set aside.
- Add the tofu to the air fryer basket and air fry at 400ºF (204ºC) for 6 mins, shaking the basket a few times during the cooking process.
- Add the vegetables back to the basket and air fry for another minute.
- Transfer the vegetables and tofu to a large bowl, add the scallions and cilantro leaves and toss with the sauce.
- Serve over rice with sesame seeds sprinkled on top.

Nutritional Facts: Cal: 200 Fat: 22 g Carbs: 60 g Protein: 80 g

5.23 Asparagus and Broccoli Green Curry

Serving: 4; **Preparation Time**: 20 mins

Cooking Time: 16 mins; **Total Time**: 36 mins

Ingredients:

- 1 (13-ounce / 369-g) can unsweetened coconut milk
- 3 tbsp. green curry paste
- 1 tbsp. soy sauce
- 1 tbsp. rice wine vinegar
- 1 tsp. honey
- 1 tsp. minced fresh ginger
- ½ onion, chopped
- 3 carrots, sliced
- 1 red bell pepper, chopped Olive oil
- 10 stalks of asparagus, cut into 2-inch pieces
- 3 cups broccoli florets
- Basmati rice for serving Fresh cilantro
- Crushed red pepper flakes (optional)

Directions:

- Combine the coconut milk, green curry paste, soy sauce, rice wine vinegar, honey and ginger in a medium saucepan and bring to a boil on the stovetop.
- Reduce the heat and simmer for 20 mins while you cook the vegetables.
- Set aside.
- Preheat the air fryer to 400°F (204°C).
- Toss the onion, carrots, and red pepper together with a little olive oil and transfer the vegetables to the air fryer basket.
- Air fry at 400°F (204°C) for 10 mins, shaking the basket a few times during the cooking process.
- Add the asparagus and broccoli florets and air fry for an additional 6 mins, again shaking the basket for even cooking.
- When the vegetables are cooked to your liking, toss them with the green curry sauce and serve in bowls over basmati rice.
- Garnish with fresh chopped cilantro and crushed red pepper flakes.

Nutritional Facts: Cal: 440 Fat: 12 g Carbs: 50 g Protein: 39 g

5.24 Lemon Spinach Rigatoni

Serving: 2 to 3; **Preparation Time**: 10 mins

Cooking Time: 13 mins; **Total Time**: 23 mins

Ingredients:

- 1 red onion, rough chopped into large chunks
- 2 tsp. olive oil, divided
- 1 bulb fennel, sliced ¼-inch thick
- ¾ cup ricotta cheese
- 1½ tsp. finely chopped lemon zest, plus more for garnish
- 1 tsp. lemon juice
- Salt and freshly ground black pepper
- 8 ounces (227 g) dried rigatoni pasta
- 3 cups baby spinach leaves

Directions:

- Bring a large stockpot of salted water to a boil on the stovetop and preheat the air fryer to 400°F (204°C).
- While the water is coming to a boil, toss the chopped onion in 1 tsp. of olive oil and transfer to the air fryer basket.
- Air fry at 400°F (204°C) for 5 mins.
- Toss the sliced fennel with 1 tsp. of olive oil and add this to the air fryer basket with the onions.
- Continue to air fry at 400°F (204°C) for 8

mins, shaking the basket a few times during the cooking process.

- Combine the ricotta cheese, lemon zest and juice, ¼ tsp. of salt and freshly ground black pepper in a bowl and stir until smooth.
- Add the dried rigatoni to the boiling water and cook according to the package directions.
- When the pasta is cooked al dente, reserve one cup of the pasta water and drain the pasta into a colander.
- Place the spinach in a serving bowl and immediately transfer the hot pasta to the bowl, wilting the spinach.
- Add the roasted onions and fennel and toss together.
- Add a little pasta water to the dish if it needs moistening.
- Then, dollop the lemon pepper ricotta cheese on top and nestle it into the hot pasta.
- Garnish with more lemon zest if desired.

Nutritional Facts: Cal: 200 Fat: 22 g Carbs: 60 g Protein: 80 g

5.25 Parmesan-Lemon Asparagus

Serving: 2; **Preparation Time**: 5 mins

Cooking Time: 5 mins; **Total Time**: 10 mins

Ingredients:

- 1 bunch asparagus, stems trimmed
- 1 tsp. olive oil
- Salt and freshly ground black pepper
- ¼ cup coarsely grated Parmesan cheese
- ½ lemon

Directions:

- Preheat the air fryer to 400°F (204°C).
- Toss the asparagus with the oil and season with salt and freshly ground black pepper.
- Transfer the asparagus to the air fryer basket and air fry at 400°F (204°C) for 5 mins, shaking the basket to turn the asparagus once or twice during the cooking process.
- When the asparagus is cooked to your liking, sprinkle the asparagus generously with the Parmesan cheese and close the air fryer drawer again.
- Let the asparagus sit for 1 minute in the turned- off air fryer.
- Then, remove the asparagus, transfer it to a serving dish and finish with a grind of black pepper and a squeeze of lemon juice.

Nutritional Facts: Cal: 300 Fat: 22 g Carbs: 89 g Protein: 100 g

5.26 Balsamic Summer Vegetables with Basil

Serving: 2; **Preparation Time**: 10 mins

Cooking Time: 37 mins; **Total Time**: 57 mins

Ingredients:

- 1 cup balsamic vinegar
- 1 zucchini, sliced
- 1 yellow squash, sliced
- 2 tbsp. olive oil
- 1 clove garlic, minced
- ½ tsp. Italian seasoning
- Salt and freshly ground black pepper
- ½ cup cherry tomatoes, halved
- 2 ounces (57 g) crumbled goat cheese
- 2 tbsp. chopped fresh basil, plus more leaves for garnish

Directions:

- Place the balsamic vinegar in a small saucepot on the stovetop.
- Bring the vinegar to a boil, lower the heat and simmer uncovered for 20 mins, until the mixture reduces and thickens. Set aside to cool.
- Preheat the air fryer to 390°F (199°C).
- Combine the zucchini and yellow squash in a large bowl.
- Add the olive oil, minced garlic, Italian seasoning, salt, and pepper and toss to coat.
- Air fries the vegetables at 390°F (199°C) for 10 mins, shaking the basket several times during the cooking process.
- Add the cherry tomatoes and continue to air fry for another 5 mins.
- Sprinkle the goat cheese over the vegetables and air fry for 2 more mins.
- Transfer the vegetables to a serving dish, drizzle with the balsamic reduction and season with freshly ground black pepper.
- Garnish with the fresh basil leaves.

Nutritional Facts: Cal: 390 Fat: 22 g Carbs: 72 g Protein: 77 g

5.27 Eggplant Bharta with Cilantro

Serving: 4; **Preparation Time**: 10 mins

Cooking Time: 20 mins; **Total Time**: 30 mins

Ingredients:

- 1 medium eggplant
- 2 tbsp. vegetable oil
- ½ cup finely minced onion
- ½ cup finely chopped fresh tomato
- 2 tbsp. fresh lemon juice
- 2 tbsp. chopped fresh cilantro
- ½ tsp. kosher salt
- ⅛ tsp. cayenne pepper

Directions:

- Rub the eggplant all over with the vegetable oil.
- Place the eggplant in the air fryer basket.
- Set the air fryer to 400°F (204°C) for 20 mins, or until the eggplant skin is blistered and charred.
- Transfer the eggplant to a resealable plastic bag, seal, and set aside for 15 to 20 mins (the eggplant will finish cooking in the residual heat trapped in the bag).
- Transfer the eggplant to a large bowl.
- Peel off and discard the charred skin.
- Roughly mash the eggplant flesh.
- Add the onion, tomato, lemon juice, cilantro, salt, and cayenne.
- Stir to combine.

Nutritional Facts: Cal: 200 Fat: 22 g Carbs: 60 g Protein: 80 g

5.28 Lettuce and Tofu Salad

Serving: 2; **Preparation Time**: 15 mins

Cooking Time: 15 mins; **Total Time**: 30 mins

Ingredients:

- For the Tofu:
- 1 tbsp. soy sauce
- 1 tbsp. vegetable oil
- 1 tsp. minced fresh ginger
- 1 tsp. minced garlic
- 8 ounces (227 g) extra-firm tofu, drained and cubed
- For the Salad:
- ¼ cup rice vinegar
- 1 tbsp. honey
- 1 tsp. salt
- 1 tsp. black pepper
- ¼ cup sliced scallions
- 1 cup julienned cucumber
- 1 cup julienned red onion
- 1 cup julienned carrots
- 6 butter lettuce leaves

Directions:

- For the tofu: In a small bowl, whisk together the soy sauce, vegetable oil, ginger, and garlic.
- Add the tofu and mix gently.
- Let stand at room temperature for 10 mins.
- Arrange the tofu in a single layer in the air fryer basket. Set the air fryer to 400°F (204°C) for 15 mins, shaking halfway through the cooking time.
- Meanwhile, for the salad: In a large bowl, whisk together the vinegar, honey, salt, pepper, and scallions.
- Add the cucumber, onion, and carrots and toss to combine.
- Set aside to marinate while the tofu cooks.
- To serve, arrange three lettuce leaves on each of two plates.
- Pile the marinated vegetables (and marinade) on the lettuce.
- Divide the tofu between the plates and serve.

Nutritional Facts: Cal: 120 Fat: 12 g Carbs: 85 g Protein: 72 g

CHAPTER 6:
Snacks & Appetizers

These delicious recipes will allow you to lose weight, improve your overall well-being, and boost your body's natural energy without having to restrict any foods.

6.1 Air Fried Cauliflower

Preparation time: 5 minutes

Cooking time: 20 minutes

Total Time: 25 minutes

Servings: 5

Ingredients:

- 16 ounces cauliflower, cut into florets
- 2/3 teaspoon salt
- ½ teaspoon ground black pepper
- 2 teaspoons olive oil
- 1 tablespoon potato starch

Directions:

- Switch on the air fryer, insert fryer basket, grease it with olive oil, then shut with its lid, set the fryer at 400 degrees F, and pre-heat for 5 minutes.
- Meanwhile, place cauliflower florets in a bowl, add remaining ingredients and toss until well coated.
- Open the fryer, add cauliflower florets in it, close with its lid and cook for 15 minutes until nicely golden and crispy, shaking the basket every 5 minutes.
- When air fryer beeps, open its lid, transfer cauliflower florets onto a serving plate and serve.

Nutrition: Calories: 36 Fat: 1 g Carbs: 5 g Protein: 1 g

6.2 Onion Rings

Preparation time: 10 minutes

Cooking time: 22 minutes

Total Time: 32 minutes

Servings: 4

Ingredients:

- 1 large white onion, peeled, sliced into ½-inch thick rings
- 2/3 cup pork rinds
- 3 tablespoons coconut flour
- 3 tablespoons almond flour
- 1/2 teaspoon garlic powder
- 1/4 teaspoon sea salt
- 1/2 teaspoon paprika
- 2 eggs

Directions:

- Take a shallow dish, place coconut flour in it, add salt, stir until mixed and set aside until required.
- Crack eggs in a bowl, whisk until combined, and set aside until required.
- Place pork rinds in another shallow dish, add almond flour in it, season with garlic powder and paprika, and stir until mixed.
- Switch on the air fryer, insert fryer basket, grease it with olive oil, then shut with its lid, set the fryer at 400 degrees F, and pre-heat for 5 minutes.
- Meanwhile, prepare onion rings and for

this, dredge them in coconut flour, dip them into beaten eggs and then coat with pork rind mixture.

- Open the fryer, add onion rings in it in a single layer, spray olive oil, close with its lid and cook for 16 minutes until nicely golden and crispy, shaking the basket every 5 minutes.

- When air fryer beeps, open its lid, transfer onion rings onto a serving plate, keep them warm and cook remaining onion rings in the same manner.

- Serve straight away.

Nutrition: Calories: 135 Fat: 7 g Carbs: 8 g Protein: 8 g

6.3 Spicy Chicken Thighs

Preparation time: 10 minutes

Cooking time: 45 minutes

Total Time: 55 minutes

Servings: 4

Ingredients:

- 2 pounds chicken thighs, bone-in, skin-on
- 2 tablespoons sliced green onions, for garnish
- 1 teaspoon toasted sesame seeds, for garnish

For the Marinade:

- 1 teaspoon minced garlic
- 2 teaspoons grated ginger
- 2 tablespoons honey
- 1/3 cup soy sauce
- 1/4 cup olive oil
- 2 tablespoons chili garlic sauce
- 1 lime, juiced

Directions:

- Prepare the marinade and for this, place

all its ingredients in a bowl and stir until combined.

- Reserve half of the marinade, then pour remaining marinade in a bowl, add chicken thighs in it, toss until well coated and marinate in the refrigerator for 30 minutes.

- Then switch on the air fryer, insert fryer basket, grease it with olive oil, then shut with its lid, set the fryer at 400 degrees F, and preheat for 5 minutes.

- Open the fryer, add chicken thighs in it in a single layer, close with its lid and cook for 20 minutes until nicely golden and crispy, turning chicken thighs halfway through.

- Meanwhile, pour remaining marinade in a saucepan, place it over medium heat, bring it to boil, and cook for 5 minutes until slightly thick, set aside until required.

- When air fryer beeps, open its lid, transfer chicken thighs onto a serving plate, keep them warm and cook remaining chicken thighs in the same manner.

- When done, brush chicken thighs generously with prepared sauce, sprinkle with green onion and sesame seeds, and serve.

Nutrition: Calories: 287 Fat: 18.8 g Carbs: 3.6 g Protein: 26.5 g

6.4 Zucchini, Yellow Squash, and Carrots

Preparation time: 10 minutes

Cooking time: 40 minutes

Total Time: 50 minutes

Servings: 4

Ingredients:

- 1 pound zucchini, ends trimmed, cut into ¾-inch half moons
- ½ pound carrots, peeled, 1-inch cubed
- 1 pound yellow squash, ends trimmed, cut into ¾-inch half moons
- 1 tablespoon chopped tarragon
- ½ teaspoon ground white pepper
- 1 teaspoon salt
- 6 teaspoons olive oil

Directions:

- Switch on the air fryer, insert fryer basket, grease it with olive oil, then shut with its lid, set the fryer at 400 degrees F, and preheat for 5 minutes.
- Meanwhile, place carrots in a bowl, drizzle with 2 teaspoon oil, and toss until combined.
- Open the fryer, add carrot pieces in it, close with its lid and cook for 5 minutes until nicely golden and crispy, shaking the basket halfway through.
- Meanwhile, place zucchini and squash pieces in a bowl, add remaining ingredients except for tarragon and toss until mixed.
- When air fryer beeps, open the lid, add zucchini and squash into fryer basket, shut with its lid and cook for 30 minutes until nicely golden and crispy, shaking the basket every 10 minutes.
- When done, transfer vegetables into a bowl, top with tarragon leaves and serve.

Nutrition: Calories: 121.5 Fat: 7.4 g Carbs: 11.5 g Protein: 2.1 g

6.5 Mac and Cheese

Preparation time: 10 minutes

Cooking time: 30 minutes

Total Time: 40 minutes

Servings: 2

Ingredients:

- 1 cup elbow macaroni, whole-wheat
- 1/2 cup broccoli florets
- ¼ teaspoon ground black pepper
- 1/3 teaspoon salt
- 1 1/2 cup grated cheddar cheese
- 1 tablespoon grated parmesan cheese
- 1/2 cup almond milk, warmed

Directions:

- Take a pot half full with water, place it over medium-high heat, bring it to boil, then add macaroni and broccoli and cook for 10 minutes until tender.
- When done, drain macaroni and vegetables, transfer them in a bowl, pour in milk, add cheddar cheese, season with black pepper and salt, and stir until well mixed.
- Switch on the air fryer, insert fryer basket, then shut with its lid, set the fryer at 350 degrees F, and preheat for 5 minutes.
- Meanwhile, place mac and cheese mixture in a heatproof baking dish that fits into the air fryer and sprinkle parmesan cheese on top.
- Open the fryer, place baking dish in it, close with its lid and cook for 15 minutes until pasta is bubbling.
- When air fryer beeps, open its lid, take out the baking dish, let the pasta sit for 10 minutes, and then serve.

Nutrition: Calories: 320 Fat: 17 g Carbs: 29 g Protein: 15 g

6.6 Whole-Wheat Pizzas

Preparation time: 10 minutes

Cooking time: 25 minutes

Total Time: 35 minutes

Servings: 2

Ingredients:

- 2 whole-wheat pita rounds
- 1 small tomato, cut into eight slices
- ½ teaspoon minced garlic
- 1 cup baby spinach leaves
- 1/4 cup marinara sauce
- 1/4 cup shredded mozzarella cheese
- 1 tablespoon grated parmesan cheese

Directions:

- Switch on the air fryer, insert fryer basket, grease it with olive oil, then shut with its lid, set the fryer at 350 degrees F, and pre-heat for 10 minutes.
- Meanwhile, prepare pizzas and for this, spread 1 tablespoon of marinara sauce on one side of each pita bread, then evenly top with spinach and tomatoes, and then sprinkle with garlic and cheeses.
- Open the fryer, add one pizza in it, close with its lid and cook for 5 minutes until nicely golden and crispy.
- When air fryer beeps, open its lid, transfer the pizza onto a serving plate, keep it warm, and cook remaining pizza in the same manner.
- Serve straight away.

Nutrition: Calories: 229 Fat: 5 g Carbs: 37 g Protein: 11 g

6.7 Chicken Nuggets

Preparation time: 10 minutes

Cooking time: 35 minutes

Total Time: 45 minutes; **Servings:** 6

Ingredients:

- 1 cup almond flour
- 2 pounds of chicken breast
- 1/2 teaspoon garlic powder
- 1 teaspoon onion flakes
- 1/2 teaspoon salt
- 4 tablespoons olive oil
- 1 egg, beaten

Directions:

- Take a shallow dish, add flour in it, season with onion powder, salt, and garlic and stir well.
- Crack the egg in a bowl, add oil, and whisk well until incorporated.
- Cut chicken breast into bite-size pieces, then dredge with almond flour mixture and coat with egg mixture.
- Switch on the air fryer, insert fryer basket, grease it with olive oil, then shut with its lid, set the fryer at 350 degrees F, and pre-heat for 5 minutes.
- Open the fryer, add chicken nuggets in it in a single layer, close with its lid and cook for 15 minutes until nicely golden and crispy, shaking the basket every 5 minutes and turning chicken nuggets halfway through.
- When air fryer beeps, open its lid, transfer chicken nuggets onto a serving plate, keep them warm and cook remaining chicken nuggets in the same manner.
- Serve straight away.

Nutrition: Calories: 445 Fat: 25.5 g Carbs: 4.5 g Protein: 48.8 g

6.8 Sweet Potato Cauliflower Patties

Preparation time: 15 minutes

Cooking time: 45 minutes

Total Time: 60 minutes

Servings: 10

Ingredients:

- 1 large sweet potato, peeled, diced
- 2 cup cauliflower florets
- 1 green onion, chopped
- 1 cup cilantro
- 1 teaspoon minced garlic
- 1/4 teaspoon salt
- 1/4 teaspoon ground black pepper
- 2 tablespoons ranch seasoning mix
- 2 tablespoons arrowroot starch
- 1/2 teaspoon red chili powder
- 1/4 cup ground flaxseed
- 1/4 teaspoon cumin
- 1/4 cup sunflower seeds

Directions:

- Place sweet potato pieces in a food processor and pulse until coarsely chopped.
- Then add cauliflower florets along with garlic and onion and pulse again until combined.
- Add remaining, pulse for 1 minute until thick batter comes together, then shape the batter into 8 to 10 patties and freeze them for 10 minutes.
- Switch on the air fryer, insert fryer basket, grease it with olive oil, then shut with its lid, set the fryer at 370 degrees F, and preheat for 5 minutes.
- Open the fryer, add prepared patties in it in a single layer, spray them with oil, close with its lid, and cook for 18 minutes until

nicely golden and crispy, turning the patties halfway through.

- When air fryer beeps, open its lid, transfer patties onto a serving plate, keep them warm and cook remaining patties in the same manner.
- Serve straight away.

Nutrition: Calories: 85 Fat: 3 g Carbs: 9 g Protein: 2.7 g

6.9 Cauliflower Rice

Preparation time: 10 minutes

Cooking time: 27 minutes

Total Time: 37 minutes

Servings: 3

Ingredients:

- 6 ounces tofu, pressed, drained
- 1/2 cup diced white onion
- 1/2 cup frozen peas
- 3 cups riced cauliflower
- 1/2 cup chopped broccoli florets
- 1 cup diced carrot
- 1 tablespoon minced ginger
- 1 teaspoon minced garlic
- 1 teaspoon turmeric powder
- 1 tablespoon apple cider vinegar
- 4 tablespoons soy sauce
- 1 1/2 teaspoons toasted sesame oil

Directions:

- Switch on the air fryer, insert fryer baking pan, grease it with olive oil, then shut with its lid, set the fryer at 370 degrees F, and preheat for 5 minutes.
- Meanwhile, place them in a large bowl, crumble it, add onion, carrot, sprinkle with turmeric, drizzle with 2 tablespoons soy sauce and toss until mixed.

- Open the fryer, add tofu in it, spray with olive oil, close with its lid and cook for 10 minutes until nicely golden, shaking the basket halfway through.
- Meanwhile, place remaining ingredients in a bowl, toss until well mixed and set aside until required.
- When air fryer beeps, open its lid, add remaining ingredients into the tofu, shake gently until just mixed, close with its lid, and cook for 12 minutes until nicely golden and cooked through, shaking the basket halfway through.
- Serve straight away.

Nutrition: Calories: 153 Fat: 4 g Carbs: 18 g Protein: 9 g

6.10 Baked Spanakopita Dip

Preparation Time: 10 minutes

Cooking time: 10 minutes

Total Time: 20 minutes

Servings: 2

Ingredients:

- Olive oil cooking spray
- 3 tablespoons olive oil, divided
- 2 tablespoons minced white onion
- 2 garlic cloves, minced
- 4 cups fresh spinach
- 4 ounces cream cheese, softened
- 4 ounces feta cheese, divided
- Zest of 1 lemon
- ¼ teaspoon ground nutmeg
- 1 teaspoon dried dill
- ½ teaspoon salt
- Pita chips, carrot sticks, or sliced bread for serving (optional)

Directions:

- Preheat the air fryer to 360°F. Coat the inside of a 6-inch ramekin or baking dish with olive oil cooking spray.
- Heat 1 tablespoon of the olive oil in a large skillet. Add the onion, then cook for 1 minute.
- Add in the garlic and cook, stirring for 1 minute more.
- Reduce the heat to low and mix in the spinach and water. Let this cook for 2 to 3 minutes, or until the spinach has wilted. Remove the skillet from the heat.
- Combine the cream cheese, 2 ounces of the feta, and the remaining 2 tablespoons of olive oil, along with the lemon zest, nutmeg, dill, and salt. In a medium bowl mix until just combined.
- Add the vegetables to the cheese base and stir until combined.
- Pour the dip mixture into the prepared ramekin and top with the remaining 2 ounces of feta cheese.
- Place the dip into the air fryer basket and cook for 10 minutes, or until heated through and bubbling.
- Serve with pita chips, carrot sticks, or sliced bread.

Nutrition: Calories: 550 Fat: 52g Protein: 14g Carbs: 9g

6.11 Coconut Hand Pies

Preparation Time: 20 minutes

Cooking time: 26 minutes

Total Time: 46 minutes

Servings: 6

Ingredients:

- 8 oz coconut flour
- 1 teaspoon vanilla extract
- 2 tablespoons Swerve
- 2 eggs, beaten
- 1 tablespoon almond butter, melted
- 1 tablespoon almond meal
- 2 tablespoons coconut shred
- Cooking spray

Directions:

- Mix coconut flour with vanilla extract, Swerve, eggs, almond butter, and almond meal.
- Knead the dough and roll it up.
- Cut the dough into squares and sprinkle with coconut shred.
- Fold the squares into the shape of pies and put in the air fryer basket.
- Sprinkle the pies with cooking spray and cook at 345F for 13 minutes per side.

Nutrition: Calories: 128 Fat: 6.5g Carbs: 11.7g Protein: 5.1g

6.12 Avocado Cream

Preparation Time: 10 minutes

Cooking time: 30 minutes

Total Time: 40 minutes

Servings: 5

Ingredients:

- 1 avocado, peeled, pitted, chopped
- 1 egg, beaten
- 2 tablespoon Erythritol
- 1 cup coconut cream
- 1 tablespoon butter, softened
- ½ teaspoon ground nutmeg

Directions:

- Blend the avocado with egg, Erythritol, coconut cream, butter, and ground nutmeg.
- When the liquid is smooth, transfer it in the ramekins.
- In the Aur Fryer basket put the ramekins and cook at 345F for 30 minutes.

Nutrition: Calories: 227 Fat: 22.5g Carbs: 6.3g Protein: 3g

6.13 Smoky Zucchini Chips

Preparation Time: 15 minutes

Cooking time: 8-10 minutes

Total Time: 25 minutes

Servings: 6

Ingredients:

- 2 large eggs
- 1 cup finely ground blanched almond flour
- ½ cup Parmesan cheese
- 1½ teaspoons sea salt
- 1 teaspoon garlic powder
- ½ teaspoon smoked paprika
- ¼ teaspoon freshly ground black pepper
- 2 zucchini, cut into ¼-inch-thick slices
- Avocado oil spray

Directions:

- The eggs are beaten in a shallow basin. Stir together the almond flour, Parmesan cheese, salt, garlic powder, smoked paprika, and black pepper in a separate basin.
- Coat the zucchini segments with the almond flour mixture after dipping them in the egg mixture.
- Adjust the temperature of the air fryer to 400 degrees Fahrenheit. Place the zucchini chips in the air fryer receptacle in a single layer, working in batches as needed. The potatoes are sprayed with oil and cooked for four minutes. Turn the chips over and drizzle them with additional oil. Cook for four to six minutes longer.
- Serve with the marinating condiment of your choice.

Nutrition: Calories: 181 Fat: 14g Carbs: 7g Protein: 11g

6.14 Avocado and Bacon Fries

Servings: 2; **Preparation Time:** 15 mins

Cooking Time: 30 mins; **Total Time:** 45 mins

Ingredients:

- 1 Egg
- 1 cup Almond flour
- 4 strips Bacon – cooked – small bits
- 2 large Avocados
- For Frying: Olive oil

Directions:

- Set the Air Fryer at 355° Fahrenheit.
- Whisk the eggs in one container.
- Add the flour with the bacon in another.
- Slice the avocado using lengthwise cuts.
- Dip into the eggs, then the flour mixture.
- Drizzle oil in the fryer tray and set the timer for 10 mins per side before serving.

Nutrition Facts: Cal: 440 Protein: 42g Carbs: 1.7g Fat 16.6g

6.15 Bacon-Wrapped Hot Dogs

Servings: 8; **Preparation Time:** 10 mins

Cooking Time: 20 mins; **Total Time:** 30 mins

Ingredients:

- 8 Bacon strips
- 8 Hot dogs

Directions:

- Wrap each hot dog with the desired amount of bacon.
- Place four hot dogs at a time in the Air Fryer basket.
- Space themso air can circulate.
- Set the fryer to 360° Fahrenheit.
- Set the timer for 15 mins.
- Check to see if they are as, you like them.
- If not, air-fry for anotherone or two mins.

Nutrition Facts: Cal: 450 Protein: 19g Carbs: 10g Fat 40g

6.16 Cheesy Hot Dogs

Servings: 2; **Preparation Time**: 5 mins

Cooking Time: 15 mins; **Total Time**: 20 mins

Ingredients:

- 2 Hot dogs
- 2 Hot dog buns
- 2 tbsp. Grated cheese

Directions:

- Heat the Air Fryer for four 4 mins at 390º Fahrenheit.
- Arrange the hot dogs in the Air Fryer and cook for five mins.
- Place the hot dog on the bun and top it off with cheese.
- Place in the fryer for about two mins to melt the cheese and serve.

Nutrition Facts: Cal: 147 Protein: 23g Carbs: 6g Fat 3g

6.17 Jalapeno Poppers

Servings: 4-5; **Preparation Time**: 2 mins

Cooking Time: 8 mins; **Total Time**: 10 mins

Ingredients:

- 10 Jalapeno peppers
- 1/4 cup Fresh parsley
- 8 oz. Cream cheese
- 3/4 cup Breadcrumbs

Directions:

- Warm the Air Fryer at 370º Fahrenheit.
- Slice the peppers into halves and deseed.
- Combine the cream cheese and half of the crumbs.
- Sprinkle in the parsley.
- Stuff each of the peppers and press the rest of the crumbs on the top for coating.
- Set the timer and air-fry for 6-8 mins or until they are nicely browned.

Nutrition Facts: Cal: 153 Protein: 5.9g Carbs: 5.7g Fat 12g

6.18 Mozzarella Cheese Sticks - Weight Watchers

Servings: 5; **Preparation Time**: 10 mins

Cooking Time: 20 mins; **Total Time**: 30 mins

Ingredients:

- 10 pieces Mozzarella string cheese
- 1 cup Italian breadcrumbs
- 1 Egg
- 5 cup Flour
- 1 cup Marinara sauce

Directions:

- Warm the Air Fryer at 400º Fahrenheit.
- Toss the breadcrumbs, salt, and pepper.
- Prepare three dishes.
- Dip each piece of cheese in flour, egg, and lastly the breadcrumbs.
- Chill the sticks for one hour to help them hold the stick shape during frying.
- Lightly spritz the sticks with coconut oil using a baking brush.
- Arrange the prepared sticks in the Air Fryer.
- Set the timer for 8 mins.
- At that point, turn them over using tongs and air-fry for another 8 mins.
- Wait for five mins and transfer them from the pan to serve.

Nutrition Facts: Cal: 128 Protein: 9.4g Carbs: 4.8g Fat 14.9g

6.19 Pigs in a Blanket

Servings: 4; **Preparation Time**: 10 mins

Cooking Time: 30 mins; **Total Time**: 40 mins

Ingredients:

- 8 oz. can Crescent rolls
- 12 oz. pkg. Cocktail franks

Directions:

- Warm the Air Fryer at 330º Fahrenheit.
- Rinse and dry the franks using paper towels.
- Slice the dough into rectangular strips 11/2 inches x 1-inch.
- Roll the dough around the franks but leave the ends open.
- Place them in the freezer for approximately five mins.
- Transfer them to the fryer for 6-8 mins.
- Raise the temperature setting to 390º Fahrenheit.
- Continue cooking for approximately three more mins.

Nutrition Facts: Cal: 60 Protein: 2g Carbs: 1g Fat 5g

6.20 Lemon-Garlic Mushrooms

Preparation Time: 10 minutes

Cooking time: 10-15 minutes

Total Time: 25 minutes

Servings: 6

Ingredients:

- 12 ounces sliced mushrooms
- 1 tablespoon avocado oil
- Sea salt
- Freshly ground black pepper
- 3 tablespoons unsalted butter
- 1 teaspoon minced garlic
- 1 teaspoon freshly squeezed lemon juice
- ½ teaspoon red pepper flakes
- 2 tablespoons chopped fresh parsley

Directions:

- Place the mushrooms in a medium bowl and toss with the oil. Season to taste with salt and pepper.
- Place the mushrooms in the air fryer basket in a single layer. Set your air fryer to 375°F and cook for 10 to 15 minutes, until the mushrooms are tender.
- While the mushrooms cook, melt the butter in a small pot or skillet over medium-low heat. Stir the garlic in and cook for 30 seconds. Take off the pot from the heat and stir in the lemon juice and red pepper flakes.
- Toss the mushrooms with the lemon-garlic butter and garnish with the parsley before serving.

Nutrition: Calories: 80 Fat: 8g Carbs: 1g Protein: 1g

6.21 Sweet Potato Fat-Free Fries

Servings: 1-2; **Preparation Time**: 10 mins

Cooking Time: 20 mins; **Total Time**: 30 mins

Ingredients:

- 1-2 Sweet potatoes
- 1-2 Red potatoes
- Optional: Parsley

Directions:

- Set the temperature to 356º Fahrenheit.
- Peel and slice the potatoes. Toss into a container of water until ready for frying.
- Towel-dry the wedges and spray using a baking oil spray.
- Arrange a single layer of fries in the basket and set the timer for ten mins.
- Give the fries a shake, return to the Air Fryer for another eight to ten mins.
- Serve them the way you like them.

Nutrition Facts: Cal: 340 Protein: 45g Carbs: 1.7g Fat 16.6g

6.22 Sweet and Spicy Pecans

Preparation Time: 7 minutes

Cooking time: 15 minutes

Total Time: 22 minutes

Servings: 8

Ingredients:

- 3 tablespoons unsalted butter, melted
- ¼ cup brown sugar substitute, such as Swerve or Sukrin Gold
- 1½ teaspoons Maldon sea salt (or regular sea salt if you like)
- ¼ teaspoon cayenne pepper, more or less to taste
- 2 cups pecan halves

Directions:

- Use parchment paper or an air fryer liner to line the basket of your air fryer.
- Add the sea salt, cayenne pepper, and brown sugar replacement to the melted butter in a small saucepan. Stir well to mix.
- Spoon the butter mixture over the pecans in a medium bowl. Coat by tossing.
- Set 275°F in the air fryer. Working in batches if required, add the pecans to the air fryer basket in a single layer and cook for 10 minutes. Cook for another 5 minutes after stirring.
- Move the pecans to a baking sheet covered with parchment paper and let them cool fully before consuming. For up to a week, keep them at room temperature in an airtight container.

Nutrition: Calories: 225 Fat: 24g Carbs: 10g Protein: 3g

6.23 Onion Rings

Preparation Time: 15 minutes

Cooking time: 10 minutes

Total Time: 25 minutes

Servings: 6

Ingredients:

- 1 large sweet onion
- 1 cup finely ground blanched almond flour
- 1 cup finely grated Parmesan cheese
- 1 tablespoon baking powder
- 1 teaspoon smoked paprika
- Sea salt
- Freshly ground black pepper
- 2 large eggs
- 1 tablespoon heavy (whipping) cream
- Avocado oil spray

Directions:

- Cut the onion crosswise into ⅓-inch-thick rings.
- In a medium bowl, mix the almond flour, baking powder, Parmesan cheese, smoked paprika, and salt and pepper to taste.
- In another medium bowl, beat the eggs and heavy cream together.
- Dip an onion ring in the egg mixture and then into the almond flour mixture. Press the almond flour mixture into the onion. Transfer to a parchment paper–lined baking sheet (I find the parchment helps reduce sticking during prep) and repeat with the remaining onion slices.
- Set the air fryer to 350°F. Arrange the onion rings in the air fryer basket in a single layer, working in batches if needed. Spray the onion rings with oil and cook for 5 minutes.

- With a spatula, carefully reach under the onions and flip them. Spray the onion rings with oil again and cook for 5 minutes more.

Nutrition: Calories: 220 Fat: 14g Carbs: 10g Protein: 14g

6.24 Garlic-Parmesan Jícama Fries

Preparation Time: 10 minutes

Cooking time: 25-35 minutes

Total Time: 40 minutes

Servings: 4

Ingredients:

- 1 medium jícama, peeled
- 1 tablespoon avocado oil
- ¼ cup (4 tablespoons) unsalted butter
- 1 tablespoon minced garlic
- ¾ teaspoon chopped dried rosemary
- ¾ teaspoon sea salt
- ½ teaspoon freshly ground black pepper
- ⅓ cup grated Parmesan cheese
- Chopped fresh parsley, for garnish
- Maldon sea salt, for garnish

Directions:

- Cut the jcama into shoestrings and 3-inch-long segments using a spiralizer or julienne peeler.
- Bring a large stockpot of water to a simmer. Cook the jcama for approximately 10 minutes. Drain, then dry with paper towels. Transfer the vegetables to a medium basin and toss with oil.
- Adjust the temperature of the air fryer to 400 degrees Fahrenheit. Layer the jcama in the receptacle in a single layer, working in batches if necessary. Checking periodically, cook for 15 to 25 minutes, until tender and golden brown.

- While the potatoes are cooking, soften the butter over a medium heat. Add the rosemary, garlic, salt, and pepper. Cook for roughly one minute.
- Toss the french potatoes with the garlic butter. The dish is topped with Parmesan cheese, parsley, and Maldon sea salt.

Nutrition: Calories: 239 Fat: 18g Carbs: 16g Protein: 5g

6.25 Lettuce Wraps

Preparation Time: 10 minutes

Cooking time: 4 minutes

Total Time: 14 minutes

Servings: 12

Ingredients:

- 12 bacon strips
- 12 lettuce leaves
- 1 tablespoon mustard
- 1 tablespoon apple cider vinegar

Directions:

- Put the bacon in the air fryer in one layer and cook at 400f for 2 minutes per side.
- Then sprinkle the bacon with mustard and apple cider vinegar and put on the lettuce.
- Wrap the lettuce into rolls.

Nutrition: Calories: 105 Fat: 9.3g Carbs: 0.5g Protein: 4.3g

6.26 Vegetable Crackers

Preparation Time: 15 minutes

Cooking time: 12 minutes

Total Time: 27 minutes

Servings: 8

Ingredients:

- 1 cup zucchini, grated
- 2 tablespoons flax meal
- 2 tablespoons coconut flour
- 1 teaspoon coconut oil
- 1 egg, beaten

Directions:

- Mix zucchini with flax meal, coconut flour, and egg.
- Roll the dough and make the crackers with the help of the cutter.
- Grease the air fryer basket with coconut oil and put the crackers inside.
- Bake them at 400F for 6 minutes per side or until they are golden brown.

Nutrition: Calories: 30 Fat: 2g Carbs: 2.3g Protein: 1.5g

6.27 Bacon-Wrapped Jalapeño Poppers

Preparation Time: 15 minutes

Cooking time: 17-22 minutes

Total Time: 37 minutes

Servings: 12

Ingredients:

- 12 jalapeño peppers
- 8 ounces cream cheese, at room temperature
- 2 tablespoons minced onion
- 1 teaspoon garlic powder
- ½ teaspoon smoked paprika
- Sea salt
- Freshly ground black pepper
- 12 strips bacon

Directions:

- Slice the jalapeños in half lengthwise, then seed them and remove any remaining white membranes to make room for the filling. Set the air fryer to 400°F. Place the jalapeños in a single layer, cut-side down, in the air fryer basket. Cook for 7 minutes.
- Remove the peppers from the air fryer and place them on a paper towel, cut-side up. Allow them to rest until they are cool enough to handle.
- While the jalapeños are cooking, in a medium bowl, stir together the cream cheese, minced onion, garlic powder, and smoked paprika. Season to taste with salt and pepper.
- Spoon the cream cheese filling into the jalapeños.
- Cut the bacon strips in half, and wrap 1 piece around each stuffed jalapeño half.
- Place the bacon-wrapped jalapeños, cut-side up, in a single layer in the air fryer basket. Cook for 10 to 15 minutes, until the bacon is crispy.

Nutrition: Calories: 116 Fat: 10g Carbs: 2g Protein: 4g

6.28 Classic Zucchini Chips

Preparation Time: 5 minutes

Cooking time: 35 minutes

Total Time: 40 minutes

Servings: 6

Ingredients:

- 3 zucchinis, thinly sliced
- 1 teaspoon salt

Directions:

- Put the zucchini in the air fryer and sprinkle with salt.
- Cook them at 350F for 35 minutes. Shake the zucchini every 5 minutes.

Nutrition: Calories: 16 Fat: 0.2g Carbs: 3.3g Protein: 1.2g

6.29 Olives Cakes

Preparation Time: 10 minutes

Cooking time: 12 minutes

Total Time: 22 minutes

Servings: 6

Ingredients:

- 2 tablespoons fresh cilantro, chopped
- 1 egg, beaten
- ½ cup coconut flour
- 1 oz scallions, chopped
- 6 oz kalamata olives, pitted and minced

Directions:

- Mix fresh cilantro with egg, coconut flour, scallions, and olives.
- Make the small cakes and put them in the air fryer on one layer.
- Cook the cakes at 385F for 6 minutes per side.

Nutrition: Calories: 85 Fat: 4.8g Carbs: 8.9g Protein: 2.6g

6.30 Pork Minis

Preparation Time: 10 minutes

Cooking time: 15 minutes

Total Time: 25 minutes; **Servings:** 4

Ingredients:

- 1 cup ground pork
- 1 teaspoon Italian seasonings
- ¼ cup Cheddar cheese, shredded
- 1 teaspoon tomato paste
- ½ teaspoon coconut oil

Directions:

- In the mixing bowl, mix ground pork with Italian seasonings, Cheddar cheese, and tomato paste.
- Then make the minis from the mixture.
- Grease the air fryer basket with coconut oil and put the pork minis inside.
- Cook them for 15 minutes at 375F.

Nutrition: Calories: 157 Fat: 6.2g Carbs: 0.5g Protein: 23.6g

6.31 Mozzarella Sticks

Preparation Time: 10 minutes

Cooking time: 4 minutes

Total Time: 14 minutes; **Servings:** 4

Ingredients:

- 1 egg, beaten
- 4 tablespoons almond flour
- 9 oz Mozzarella, cut into sticks

Directions:

- Dip the mozzarella sticks in the egg and them coat in the almond flour.
- Then put the mozzarella sticks in the air fryer basket and cook at 400F for 4 minutes.

Nutrition: Calories: 238 Fat: 15.7g Carbs: 3.8g Protein: 20.9g

6.32 Kale Chips

Preparation Time: 10 minutes
Cooking time: 10-14 minutes
Total Time: 24 minutes
Servings: 8
Ingredients:

- 1 bunch kale, washed, stemmed, and torn into pieces
- 1 tablespoon extra-virgin olive oil
- 2 teaspoons everything seasoning (see Ingredient Tip)

Directions:

- Place the kale leaves in a large bowl. Toss with the olive oil and seasoning.
- Arrange half of the kale in the air fryer basket. Set the air fryer to 325°F. Cook for 5 to 7 minutes, shaking halfway through, until the kale is crispy. Repeat with the remaining kale.

Nutrition: Calories: 35 Fat: 2g Carbs: 3g Protein: 1g

6.33 Rosemary Balls

Preparation Time: 5 minutes
Cooking time: 12 minutes
Total Time: 17 minutes
Servings: 6
Ingredients:

- ¼ teaspoon ground black pepper
- 1 ½ cup almond flour
- 1 teaspoon garlic powder
- 1 teaspoon dried rosemary
- 2 eggs, beaten
- 1 cup mushrooms, diced

Directions:

- In the mixing bowl, mix almond flour with garlic powder, dried rosemary, eggs, and mushrooms.
- Make the balls and put them in the air fryer.
- Cook the meal at 360F for 12 minutes.

Nutrition: Calories: 68 Fat: 4.9g Carbs: 2.5g Protein: 3.8g

6.34 Seaweed Crisps

Preparation Time: 10 minutes
Cooking time: 5 minutes
Total Time: 15 minutes
Servings: 4
Ingredients:

- 3 nori sheets
- 1 teaspoon nutritional yeast
- 2 tablespoons water

Directions:

- Cut the nori sheets roughly and put in the air fryer basket.
- Sprinkle the nori sheets with water and nutritional yeast and cook at 375F for 5 minutes.

Nutrition: Calories: 4 Fat: 0.1g Carbs: 0.6g Protein: 0.8g

6.35 French Fries

Servings: 2; **Preparation Time:** 5 mins

Cooking Time: 15 mins; **Total Time:** 20 mins

Ingredients:

- Egg (1)
- Almond flour (1 cup)
- Bacon – cooked – small bits (4 strips)
- Avocados (2 large)
- For Frying: Olive oil

Directions:

- Set the Air Fryer at 355° Fahrenheit.
- Whisk the eggs in one container. Add the flour with the bacon in another.
- Slice the avocado using lengthwise cuts. Dip into the eggs, then the flour mixture.
- Drizzle oil in the fryer tray and set the timer for 10 mins per side before serving.

Nutrition Facts: Cal: 60 Protein: 2g Carbs: 1g Fat 5g

6.36 German Hot Dogs

Servings: 8; **Preparation Time:** 5 mins

Cooking Time: 15 mins; **Total Time:** 20 mins

Ingredients:

- Bacon strips (8)
- Hot dogs (8)

Directions:

- Wrap each hot dog with the desired amount of bacon.
- Place four hot dogs at a time in the Air Fryer basket. Space them so air can circulate.
- Set the fryer to 360 ° Fahrenheit. Set the timer for 15 mins.

- Check to see if they are as you like them. If not, air-fry for another one or two mins.

Nutrition Facts: Cal: 110 Protein: 9g Carbs: 1g Fat 8g

6.37 David's Dogs

Servings: 2; **Preparation Time:** 5 mins

Cooking Time: 15 mins; **Total Time:** 20 mins

Ingredients:

- Hot dogs (2)
- Hot dog buns (2)
- Grated cheese (2 tbsp.)

Directions:

- Heat the Air Fryer for four (4) mins at 390° Fahrenheit.
- Arrange the hot dogs in the Air Fryer and cook for five mins.
- Place the hot dog on the bun and top it off with cheese.
- Place in the fryer for about two mins to melt the cheese and serve.

Nutrition Facts: Cal: 450 Protein: 19g Carbs: 10g Fat 40g

6.38 Herbed Popper

Servings: 4-5; **Preparation Time:** 5 mins

Cooking Time: 6-8 mins; **Total Time:** 11 mins

Ingredients:

- Jalapeno peppers (10)
- Fresh parsley (.25 cup)
- Cream cheese (8 oz.)
- Breadcrumbs (.75 cup)

Directions:

- Warm the Air Fryer at 370° Fahrenheit.
- Slice the peppers into halves and deseed.
- Combine the cream cheese and half of the

crumbs. Sprinkle in the parsley.

- Stuff each of the peppers and press the rest of the crumbs on the top for coating.
- Set the timer and air-fry for 6-8 mins or until they are nicely browned.

Nutritional Facts: Cal: 200 Fat: 22 g Carbs: 60 g Protein: 80 g

6.39 Cheesy Breadsticks

Servings: 5; **Preparation Time**: 5 mins

Cooking Time: 13 mins; **Total Time**: 18 mins

Ingredients:

- Mozzarella string cheese (10 pieces)
- Italian breadcrumbs (1 cup)
- Egg (1)
- Flour (.5 cup)
- Marinara sauce (1 cup)

Directions:

- Warm the Air Fryer at 400° Fahrenheit.
- Toss the breadcrumbs, salt, and pepper.
- Prepare three dishes. Dip each piece of cheese in flour, egg, and lastly the breadcrumbs.
- Chill the sticks for one hour to help them hold the stick shape during frying.
- Lightly spritz the sticks with coconut oil using a baking brush.
- Arrange the prepared sticks in the Air Fryer. Set the timer for 8 mins. At that point, turn them over using tongs and air-fry for another 8 mins.
- Wait for five mins and transfer them from the pan to serve.

Nutritional Facts: Cal: 300 Fat: 22 g Carbs: 89 g Protein: 100 g

6.40 Pork Bites

Servings: 4; **Preparation Time**: 5 mins

Cooking Time: 6-8 mins; **Total Time**: 17 mins

Ingredients:

- Crescent rolls (8 oz. can)
- Cocktail franks (12 oz. pkg.)

Directions:

- Warm the Air Fryer at 330° Fahrenheit.
- Rinse and dry the franks using paper towels.
- Slice the dough into rectangular strips (1.5 inches x 1-inch).
- Roll the dough around the franks, but leave the ends open.
- Place them in the freezer for approximately five mins. T
- Transfer them to the fryer for 6-8 mins.
- Raise the temperature setting to 390° Fahrenheit. Continue cooking for approximately three more mins.

Nutrition Facts: Cal: 450 Protein: 19g Carbs: 10g Fat 40g

6.41 Avocado Sticks

Preparation Time: 10 minutes

Cooking time: 14 minutes

Total Time: 24 minutes

Servings: 4

Ingredients:

- 1 avocado, pitted, halves
- 1 egg, beaten
- 1 tablespoon coconut shred

Directions:

- Cut the avocado halves into 4 wedges and dip in the egg.
- Then coat the avocado in coconut shred and put in the air fryer.
- Cook the avocado sticks at 375F for 7 minutes per side.

Nutrition: Calories: 131 Fat: 12.1g Carbs: 4.9g Protein: 2.3g

6.42 Crispy Frics

Servings: 1-2; **Preparation Time:** 5 mins

Cooking Time: 10 mins; **Total Time:** 15 mins

Ingredients:

- Sweet potatoes (1-2)
- Red potatoes (1-2)
- Optional: Parsley

Directions:

- Set the temperature to 356° Fahrenheit.
- Peel and slice the potatoes. Toss into a container of water until ready for frying.
- Towel-dry the wedges and spray using a baking oil spray.
- Arrange a single layer of fries in the basket and set the timer for ten mins.
- Give the fries a shake, return to the Air Fryer for another eight to ten mins.
- Serve them the way you like them.

Nutrition Facts: Cal: 128 Protein: 9.4g Carbs: 4.8g Fat 14.9g

CHAPTER 7:
Beans and Grains

7.1 Black Bean and Sweet Potato Burgers

Serving: 4; **Preparation Time**: 10 mins

Cooking Time: 10 mins; **Total Time**: 20 mins

Ingredients:

- 1 (15-ounce / 425-g) can black beans, drained and rinsed
- 1 cup mashed sweet potato
- ½ tsp. dried oregano
- ¼ tsp. dried thyme
- ¼ tsp. dried marjoram
- 1 garlic clove, minced
- ¼ tsp. salt
- ¼ tsp. black pepper
- 1 tbsp. lemon juice 1 cup cooked brown rice
- ¼ to ½ cup whole wheat breadcrumbs
- 1 tbsp. olive oil

Directions:

- Whole wheat buns or whole wheat pitas Plain Greek yogurt
- Avocado Lettuce Tomato Red onion
- Preheat the air fryer to 380°F (193°C).
- In a large bowl, use the back of a fork to mash the black beans until there are no large pieces left.
- Add the mashed sweet potato, oregano, thyme, marjoram, garlic, salt, pepper, and lemon juice, and mix until well combined.
- Stir in the cooked rice.
- Add in ¼ cup of the whole wheat breadcrumbs and stir.
- Check to see if the mixture is dry enough to form patties.
- If it seems too wet and loose, add an additional ¼ cup breadcrumbs and stir.
- Form the dough into 4 patties. Place them into the air fryer basket in a single layer, making sure that they don't touch each other.
- Brush half of the olive oil onto the patties and bake for 5 mins.
- Flip the patties over, brush the other side with the remaining oil, and bake for an additional 4 to 5 mins.
- Serve on toasted whole wheat buns or whole wheat pitas with a spoonful of yogurt and avocado, lettuce, tomato, and red onion as desired.

Nutritional Facts: Cal: 200 Fat: 22 g Carbs: 60 g Protein: 80 g

7.2 Red Lentil-Veggie Patties

Serving: 4; **Preparation Time**: 15 mins

Cooking Time: 10 mins; **Total Time**: 25 mins

Ingredients:

- 1 cup cooked brown lentils
- ¼ cup fresh parsley leaves
- ½ cup shredded carrots
- ¼ red onion, minced
- ¼ red bell pepper, minced
- 1 jalapeño, seeded and minced
- 2 garlic cloves, minced
- 1 egg
- 2 tbsp. lemon juice
- 2 tbsp. olive oil, divided
- ½ tsp. onion powder
- ½ tsp. smoked paprika
- ½ tsp. dried oregano
- ¼ tsp. salt
- ¼ tsp. black pepper
- ½ cup whole wheat breadcrumbs Whole wheat buns or whole wheat pitas Plain Greek yogurt
- Tomato
- Lettuce Red Onion

Directions:

- Preheat the air fryer to 380°F (193°C).
- In a food processor, pulse the lentils and parsley mostly smooth.
- Pour the lentils into a large bowl, and combine with the carrots, onion, bell pepper, jalapeño, garlic, egg, lemon juice, and 1 tbsp. olive oil.
- Add the onion powder, paprika, oregano, salt, pepper, and breadcrumbs. Stir everything together until the seasonings and breadcrumbs are well distributed.
- Form the dough into 4 patties.

- Place them into the air fryer basket in a single layer, making sure that they don't touch each other.
- Brush the remaining 1 tbsp. of olive oil over the patties.
- Bake for 5 mins.
- Flip the patties over and bake for an additional 5 mins.
- Serve on toasted whole wheat buns or whole wheat pitas with a spoonful of yogurt and lettuce, tomato, and red onion as desired.

Nutritional Facts: Cal: 200 Fat: 22 g Carbs: 60 g Protein: 80 g

7.3 Goat Cheese and Red Lentil Stuffed Tomatoes

Serving: 4

Preparation Time: 10 mins

Cooking Time: 15 mins

Total Time: 25 mins

Ingredients:

- 4 tomatoes
- ½ cup cooked red lentils
- 1 garlic clove, minced
- 1 tbsp. minced red onion
- 4 basil leaves, minced
- ¼ tsp. salt
- ¼ tsp. black pepper
- 4 ounces (113 g) goat cheese
- 2 tbsp. shredded Parmesan cheese

Directions:

- Preheat the air fryer to 380°F (193°C).
- Slice the top off each tomato.
- Using a knife and spoon, cut and scoop out half of the flesh inside of the tomato.
- Place it into a medium bowl.

- To the bowl with the tomato, add the cooked lentils, garlic, onion, basil, salt, pepper, and goat cheese. Stir until well combined.
- Spoon the filling into the scooped-out cavity of each of the tomatoes, then top each one with ½ tbsp. of shredded Parmesan cheese.
- Place the tomatoes in a single layer in the air fryer basket and bake for 15 mins.

Nutritional Facts: Cal: 200 Fat: 22 g Carbs: 60 g Protein: 80 g

7.4 Green Lentil and Brown Rice Balls

Serving: 6

Preparation Time: 5 mins

Cooking Time: 11 mins

Total Time: 16 mins

Ingredients:

- ½ cup cooked green lentils
- 2 garlic cloves, minced
- ¼ white onion, minced
- ¼ cup parsley leaves
- 5 basil leaves
- 1 cup cooked brown rice
- 1 tbsp. lemon juice
- 1 tbsp. olive oil
- ½ tsp. salt

Directions:

- Preheat the air fryer to 380°F (193°C).
- In a food processor, pulse the cooked lentils with the garlic, onion, parsley, and basil until mostly smooth. (You will want some bits of lentils in the mixture.)
- Pour the lentil mixture into a large bowl, and stir in brown rice, lemon juice, olive oil, and salt. Stir until well combined.

- Form the rice mixture into 1-inch balls.
- Place the rice balls in a single layer in the air fryer basket, making sure that they don't touch each other.
- Fry for 6 mins. Turn the rice balls and then fry for an additional 4 to 5 mins, or until browned on all sides.

Nutritional Facts: Cal: 230 Fat: 20 g Carbs: 97 g Protein: 65 g

7.5 White Beans with Garlic and Peppers

Serving: 4

Preparation Time: 5 mins

Cooking Time: 15 mins

Total Time: 20 mins

Ingredients:

- Olive oil cooking spray
- (15-ounce / 425-g) cans white beans, or cannellini beans, drained and rinsed
- 1 red bell pepper, diced
- ½ red onion, diced
- 3 garlic cloves, minced
- 1 tbsp. olive oil
- ¼ to ½ tsp. salt
- ½ tsp. black pepper
- 1 rosemary sprig
- 1 bay leaf

Directions:

- Preheat the air fryer to 360°F (182°C).
- Lightly coat the inside of a 5-cup capacity casserole dish with olive oil cooking spray.
- In a large bowl, combine the beans, bell pepper, onion, garlic, olive oil, salt, and pepper.
- Pour the bean mixture into the prepared casserole dish, place the rosemary and bay

leaf on top, and then place the casserole dish into the air fryer.

- Roast for 15 mins.
- Remove the rosemary and bay leaves, then stir well before serving.

Nutritional Facts: Cal: 300 Fat: 22 g Carbs: 89 g Protein: 100 g

7.6 Balsamic Two-Beans with Dill

Serving: 4; **Preparation Time**: 5 mins

Cooking Time: 30 mins; **Total Time**: 35 mins

Ingredients:

- Olive oil cooking spray
- 1 (15-ounce / 425-g) can cannellini beans, drained and rinsed
- 1 (15-ounce / 425-g) can great northern beans, drained and rinsed
- ½ yellow onion, diced
- (8-ounce / 227-g) can tomato sauce
- 1½ tbsp. honey
- ¼ cup olive oil
- 2 garlic cloves, minced
- 2 tbsp. chopped fresh dill
- ½ tsp. salt
- ½ tsp. black pepper
- 1 bay leaf
- 1 tbsp. balsamic vinegar
- 2 ounces (57 g) feta cheese, crumbled, for serving

Directions:

- Preheat the air fryer to 360ºF (182ºC).
- Lightly coat the inside of a 5-cup capacity casserole dish with olive oil cooking spray.
- In a large bowl, combine all ingredients except the feta cheese and stir until well combined.
- Pour the bean mixture into the prepared casserole dish.

- Bake in the air fryer for 30 mins.
- Remove from the air fryer and remove and discard the bay leaf. Sprinkle crumbled feta over the top before serving.

Nutritional Facts: Cal: 120 Fat: 12 g Carbs: 85 g Protein: 72 g

7.7 Pearl Barley and Mushroom Pilaf

Serving: 4; **Preparation Time**: 5 mins;

Cooking Time: 37 mins; **Total Time**: 42 mins

Ingredients:

- Olive oil cooking spray
- 2 tbsp. olive oil
- 8 ounces (227 g) button mushrooms, diced
- ½ yellow onion, diced
- 2 garlic cloves, minced
- 1 cup pearl barley
- 2 cups vegetable broth
- 1 tbsp. fresh thyme, chopped
- ½ tsp. salt
- ¼ tsp. smoked paprika Fresh parsley, for garnish

Directions:

- Preheat the air fryer to 380ºF (193ºC).
- Lightly coat the inside of a 5-cup capacity casserole dish with olive oil cooking spray.
- In a large skillet, heat the olive oil over medium heat.
- Add the mushrooms and onion and cook, stirring occasionally, for 5 mins, or until the mushrooms begin to brown.
- Add the garlic and cook for an additional 2 mins.
- Transfer the vegetables to a large bowl.
- Add the barley, broth, thyme, salt, and paprika.
- Pour the barley-and-vegetable mixture

into the prepared casserole dish and place the dish into the air fryer.

- Bake for 15 mins.
- Stir the barley mixture.
- Reduce the heat to 360°F (182°C), then return the barley to the air fryer and bake for 15 mins more.
- Remove from the air fryer and let sit for 5 mins before fluffing with a fork and topping with fresh parsley.

Nutritional Facts: Cal: 200 Fat: 22 g Carbs: 60 g Protein: 80 g

7.8 Chickpea and Brown Rice Bake

Serving: 6; **Preparation Time**: 10 mins

Cooking Time: 45 mins; **Total Time**: 55 mins

Ingredients:

- Olive oil cooking spray
- 1 cup long-grain brown rice
- 2¼ cups chicken stock
- 1 (15½-ounce / 439-g) can chickpeas, drained and rinsed
- ½ cup diced carrot
- ½ cup green peas
- 1 tsp. ground cumin
- ½ tsp. ground turmeric
- ½ tsp. ground ginger
- ½ tsp. onion powder
- ½ tsp. salt
- ¼ tsp. ground cinnamon
- ¼ tsp. garlic powder
- ¼ tsp. black pepper Fresh parsley, for garnish

Directions:

- Preheat the air fryer to 380°F (193°C).
- Lightly coat the inside of a 5-cup capacity casserole dish with olive oil cooking spray.
- In the casserole dish, combine the rice,

stock, chickpeas, carrot, peas, cumin, turmeric, ginger, onion powder, salt, cinnamon, garlic powder, and black pepper.

- Stir well to combine.
- Cover loosely with aluminum foil.
- Place the covered casserole dish into the air fryer and bake for 20 mins.
- Remove from the air fryer and stir well.
- Place the casserole back into the air fryer, uncovered, and bake for 25 mins more.
- Fluff with a spoon and sprinkle with fresh chopped parsley before serving.

Nutritional Facts: Cal: 220 Fat: 12 g Carbs: 45 g Protein: 80 g

7.9 Buckwheat, Potato and Carrot Bake

Serving: 6; **Preparation Time**: 15 mins

Cooking Time: 30 mins; **Total Time**: 45 mins

Ingredients:

- Olive oil cooking spray
- 2 large potatoes, cubed
- 2 carrots, sliced
- 1 small rutabaga, cubed
- 2 celery stalks, chopped
- ½ tsp. smoked paprika
- ¼ cup plus 1 tbsp. olive oil, divided
- 2 rosemary sprigs
- 1 cup buckwheat groats
- 2 cups vegetable broth
- 2 garlic cloves, minced
- ½ yellow onion, chopped
- 1 tsp. salt

Directions:

- Preheat the air fryer to 380°F (193°C).
- Lightly coat the inside of a 5-cup capacity casserole dish with olive oil cooking spray.

- In a large bowl, toss the potatoes, carrots, rutabaga, and celery with the paprika and ¼ cup olive oil.
- Pour the vegetable mixture into the prepared casserole dish and top with the rosemary sprigs.
- Place the casserole dish into the air fryer and bake for 15 mins.
- While the vegetables are cooking, rinse and drain the buckwheat groats.
- In a medium saucepan over medium-high heat, combine the groats, vegetable broth, garlic, onion, and salt with the remaining 1 tbsp. olive oil.
- Bring the mixture to a boil, then reduce the heat to low, cover, and cook for 10 to 12 mins.
- Remove the casserole dish from the air fryer.
- Remove the rosemary sprigs and discard.
- Pour the cooked buckwheat into the dish with the vegetables and stir to combine.
- Cover with aluminum foil and bake for an additional 15 mins.
- Stir before serving.

Nutritional Facts: Cal: 200 Fat: 22 g Carbs: 60 g Protein: 80 g

7.10 Butter Bean Bake with Tomatoes

Serving: 4; **Preparation Time**: 5 mins

Cooking Time: 30 mins; **Total Time**: 35 mins

Ingredients:

- Olive oil cooking spray
- (15-ounce / 425-g) can cooked butter beans, drained, and rinsed
- 1 cup diced fresh tomatoes
- ½ tbsp. tomato paste
- 2 garlic cloves, minced
- ½ yellow onion, diced
- ½ tsp. salt
- ¼ cup olive oil
- ¼ cup fresh parsley, chopped

Directions:

- Preheat the air fryer to 380ºF (193ºC).
- Lightly coat the inside of a 5-cup capacity casserole dish with olive oil cooking spray.
- In a large bowl, combine the butter beans, tomatoes, tomato paste, garlic, onion, salt, and olive oil, mixing until all ingredients are combined.
- Pour the mixture into the prepared casserole dish and top with the chopped parsley.
- Bake in the air fryer for 15 mins. Stir well, then return to the air fryer and bake for 15 mins more.

Nutritional Facts: Cal: 332 Fat: 26 g Carbs: 89 g Protein: 54

7.11 Green Peas and Cauliflower Bake

Serving: 8; **Preparation Time**: 5 mins

Cooking Time: 25 mins; **Total Time**: 30 mins

Ingredients:

- 1 cup cauliflower florets, fresh or frozen
- ½ white onion, roughly chopped
- 2 tbsp. olive oil
- ½ cup unsweetened almond milk
- 3 cups green peas, fresh or frozen
- 3 garlic cloves, minced
- 2 tbsp. fresh thyme leaves, chopped
- 1 tsp. fresh rosemary leaves, chopped
- ½ tsp. salt
- ½ tsp. black pepper
- Shredded Parmesan cheese, for garnish
- Fresh parsley, for garnish

Directions:

- Preheat the air fryer to 380°F (193°C).
- In a large bowl, combine the cauliflower florets and onion with the olive oil and toss well to coat.
- Put the cauliflower-and-onion mixture into the air fryer basket in an even layer and bake for 15 mins.
- Transfer the cauliflower and onion to a food processor. Add the almond milk and pulse until smooth.
- In a medium saucepan, combine the cauliflower puree, peas, garlic, thyme, rosemary, salt, and pepper and mix well.
- Cook over medium heat for an additional 10 mins, stirring regularly.
- Serve with a sprinkle of Parmesan cheese and chopped fresh parsley.

Nutritional Facts: Cal: 133 Fat: 54 g Carbs: 8 g Protein: 70 g

7.12 Parmesan Farro Risotto with Sage

Serving: 6; **Preparation Time**: 5 mins

Cooking Time: 35 mins; **Total Time**: 40 mins

Ingredients:

- Olive oil cooking spray
- 1½ cups uncooked farro
- 2½ cups chicken broth
- 1 cup tomato sauce
- 1 yellow onion, diced
- 3 garlic cloves, minced
- 1 tbsp. fresh sage, chopped
- ½ tsp. salt
- 2 tbsp. olive oil
- 1 cup Parmesan cheese, grated, divided

Directions:

- Preheat the air fryer to 380°F (193°C).

- Lightly coat the inside of a 5-cup capacity casserole dish with olive oil cooking spray.
- In a large bowl, combine the farro, broth, tomato sauce, onion, garlic, sage, salt, olive oil, and ½ cup of the Parmesan.
- Pour the farro mixture into the prepared casserole dish and cover with aluminum foil.
- Bake for 20 mins, then uncover and stir.
- Sprinkle the remaining
- ½ cup Parmesan over the top and bake for 15 mins more.
- Stir well before serving.

Nutritional Facts: Cal: 120 Fat: 12 g Carbs: 85 g Protein: 72 g

7.13 Red Lentils and Onions with Lemon

Serving: 4; **Preparation Time**: 10 mins

Cooking Time: 45 mins; **Total Time**: 55 mins

Ingredients:

- 1 cup red lentils 4 cups water
- Cooking oil spray
- 1 medium-size onion, peeled and cut into
- ¼-inch-thick rings Sea salt
- ½ cup kale, stems removed, thinly sliced
- 3 large garlic cloves, pressed or minced
- 2 tbsp. fresh lemon juice
- 2 tsp. nutritional yeast
- 1 tsp. sea salt
- 1 tsp. lemon zest
- ¾ tsp. freshly ground black pepper

Directions:

- In a medium-large pot, bring the lentils and water to a boil over medium-high heat.
- Reduce the heat to low and simmer, uncovered, for about 30 mins (or until the

lentils have dissolved completely), making sure to stir every 5 mins or so as they cook (so that the lentils don't stick to the bottom of the pot).

- While the lentils are cooking, get the rest of your dish together.
- Spray the air fryer basket with oil and place the onion rings inside, separating them as much as possible. Spray them with the oil and sprinkle with a little salt.
- Fry at 390°F (199°C) for 5 mins.
- Remove the air fryer basket, shake, or stir, spray again with oil, and fry for another 5 mins.
- Remove the air fryer basket, spray the onions again with oil, and fry for a final 5 mins or until all the pieces are crisp and browned.
- To finish the lentils: Add the kale to the hot lentils, and stir very well, as the heat from the lentils will steam the thinly sliced greens.
- Stir in the garlic, lemon juice, nutritional yeast, salt, zest, and pepper.
- Stir very well and then distribute evenly in bowls. Top with the crisp onion rings and serve.

Nutritional Facts: Cal: 200 Fat: 22 g Carbs: 60 g Protein: 80 g

7.14 Garlic Pinto Bean

Serving: 2; **Preparation Time**: 5 mins

Cooking Time: 8 mins; **Total Time**: 13 mins

Ingredients:

- (15-ounce / 425-g) can pinto beans, drained
- ¼ cup tomato sauce
- 2 tbsp. nutritional yeast
- 2 large garlic cloves, pressed or minced
- ½ tsp. dried oregano
- ½ tsp. cumin
- ¼ tsp. sea salt
- ⅛ tsp. freshly ground black pepper
- Cooking oil spray

Directions:

- In a medium bowl, stir together the beans, tomato sauce, nutritional yeast, garlic, oregano, cumin, salt, and pepper until well combined.
- Spray the 6-inch round, 2-inch-deep baking pan with oil and pour the bean mixture into it. Bake at 390°F (199°C) for 4 mins.
- Remove, stir well, and bake for another 4 mins, or until the mixture has thickened and is heated through.
- It will most likely form a little crust on top and be lightly browned in spots.
- Serve hot.
- This will keep, refrigerated in an airtight container, for up to a week.

Nutritional Facts: Cal: 200 Fat: 22 g Carbs: 60 g Protein: 80 g

CHAPTER 8:
Pork & Lamb Options

8.1 Bacon-Wrapped Pork Tenderloin

Servings: 4-6 **Preparation Time**: 5 mins

Cooking Time: 15 mins ; **Total Time**: 20 mins

Ingredients:

- 1 lb. Pork tenderloin
- 1-2 tbsp. Dijon mustard
- 3-4 strips Bacon

Directions:

- Set the Air Fryer temperature at 360° Fahrenheit.
- Coat the tenderloin with the mustard and wrap with the bacon.
- Air-fry them for 15 mins.
- Flip and cook 10 to 15 more mins.
- Serve with your favorite sides.

Nutrition Facts: Cal: 396 Protein: 59.6g Carbs: 1g Fat 15.6g

8.2 Bratwurst and Veggies

Servings: 6; **Preparation Time**: 5 mins

Cooking Time: 20 mins ; **Total Time**: 25 mins

Ingredients:

- 5 links/1 pkg. Bratwurst Approx.
- 1 each red and green bell pepper
- 1/4 cup Onion - red or purple
- 1/2 tbsp. Gluten-free Cajun seasoning

Directions:

- Warm the unit to reach 390° Fahrenheit.
- Line the Air Fryer with foil, if preferred.
- Slice and add in the vegetables.
- Slice the bratwurst into about 01/2-inch size rounds, and place on top of the veggies.
- Evenly sprinkle the seasoning on top.
- Air-fry for 10 mins.
- Carefully open and stir or mix.
- Air-fry for another 10 mins before serving.

Nutrition Facts: Cal: 340 Protein: 45g Carbs: 1.7g Fat 16.6g

8.3 Crispy Dumplings

Servings: 2; **Preparation Time**: 5 mins

Cooking Time: 10 mins ; **Total Time**: 15 mins

Ingredients:

- 1/2 lb. Ground pork
- 1 tbsp. Olive oil
- 1/2 tsp. each Black pepper and salt
- 1 pkg. Dumpling wrappers

Directions:

- Set the Air Fryer temperature setting at 390° Fahrenheit.
- Mix the fixings together.
- Prepare each dumpling using two teaspoons of the pork mixture.
- Seal the edges with a portion of water to make the triangle form.
- Lightly spritz the Air Fryer basket using a cooking oil spray as needed.
- Add the dumplings to air-fry for eight mins.
- Serve when they're ready.

Nutrition Facts: Cal: 450 Protein: 19g Carbs: 10g Fat 40g

8.4 Pork Taquitos

Servings: 10; **Preparation Time**: 10 mins

Cooking Time: 10 mins; **Total Time**: 20 mins

Ingredients:

- 3 cups of Cooked pork chicken or tenderloin, shredded
- 2 and 1/2 cups of Fat-free shredded mozzarella
- 10 Flour tortillas, small
- 1 lime juice

Directions:

- Set the Air Fryer at 380° Fahrenheit.
- Sprinkle the juice over the pork.
- Microwave five of the tortillas at a time putting a damp paper towel over them for 10 seconds.
- Add three ounces of pork and
- ¼ of a cup of cheese to each tortilla.
- Tightly roll the tortillas. Line the tortillas onto a greased foil- lined pan.
- Spray an even coat of cooking oil spray over the tortillas.
- Air Fry for 7 to 10 mins or until the tortillas are a golden color, flipping halfway through.

Nutrition Facts: Cal: 147 Protein: 23g Carbs: 6g Fat 3g

8.5 Ranch-Style Pork Chops

Servings: 4; **Preparation Time**: 10 mins

Cooking Time: 15 mins ; **Total Time**: 25 mins

Ingredients:

- chops 4 Center-cut - 1-inch boneless pork
- 2 tsp. Dry ranch salad dressing mix - ex. Hidden Valley
- Also Needed: Aluminum foil and cooking oil spray

Directions:

- Warm the Air Fryer to 390° Fahrenheit.
- Lightly spray both sides of the chops and the inside of the Air Fryer basket using a cooking oil spray.
- Sprinkle both sides with the ranch seasoning mix and let it rest at room temperature for ten mins.
- Place the chops in the Air Fryer, working in batches, if necessary, to ensure the fryer isn't overcrowded.
- Cook for five mins.
- Flip the chops and cook five mins more.
- Let it rest on a foil-covered plate for an additional five mins before serving.

Nutrition Facts: Cal: 450 Protein: 19g Carbs: 10g Fat 40g

8.6 Bacon-Wrapped Pork Tenderloin

Servings: 4-6; **Preparation Time**: 15 mins

Cooking Time: 30 mins; **Total Time**: 45 mins

Ingredients:

- 1 lb. Pork tenderloin
- 1-2 tbsp. Dijon mustard
- 3-4 strips Bacon

Directions:

- Set the Air Fryer temperature at 360° Fahrenheit.
- Coat the tenderloin with the mustard and wrap with the bacon.
- Air-fry them for 15 mins.
- Flip and cook 10 to 15 more mins.
- Serve with your favorite sides.

Nutrition Facts: Cal: 450 Protein: 19g Carbs: 10g Fat 40g

8.7 Bratwurst and Veggies

Servings: 6; **Preparation Time**: 5 mins

Cooking Time: 20 mins; **Total Time**: 25 mins

Ingredients:

- 5 links/1 pkg. Bratwurst Approx.
- 1 each red and green bell pepper
- 1/4 cup of Onion - red or purple
- 1/2 tbsp. of Gluten-free Cajun seasoning

Directions:

- Warm the unit to reach 390° Fahrenheit.
- Line the Air Fryer with foil, if preferred.
- Slice and add in the vegetables.
- Slice the bratwurst into about 01/2-inch size rounds, and place on top of the veggies.
- Evenly sprinkle the seasoning on top.
- Air-fry for 10 mins. Carefully open and stir or mix.
- Air-fry for another 10 mins before serving.

Nutrition Facts: Cal: 450 Protein: 19g Carbs: 10g Fat 40g

8.8 Crispy Dumplings

Servings: 2; **Preparation Time**: 10 mins

Cooking Time: 10 mins; **Total Time**: 20 mins

Ingredients:

- 1/2 lb. Ground pork
- 1 tbsp. Olive oil
- 1/2 tsp. each Black pepper and salt
- half of 1 pkg Dumpling wrappers.

Directions:

- Set the Air Fryer temperature setting at 390° Fahrenheit.
- Mix the fixings together.
- Prepare each dumpling using two teaspoons of the pork mixture.
- Seal the edges with a portion of water to make the triangle form.
- Lightly spritz the Air Fryer basket using a cooking oil spray as needed.
- Add the dumplings to air-fry for eight mins.
- Serve when they're ready.

Nutrition Facts: Cal: 60 Protein: 2g Carbs: 1g Fat 5g

8.9 Southern Fried Pork Chops

Servings: 5; **Preparation Time**: 30 mins

Cooking Time: 25 mins; **Total Time**: 55 mins

Ingredients:

- 4 Pork chops
- 3 tbsp. Buttermilk
- 1/4 cup All-purpose flour
- Seasoning salt
- Freshly cracked black pepper as desired

Directions:

- Set the fryer at 380° Fahrenheit.
- Rinse and dry the chops using a paper towel.
- Season using the pepper and seasoning salt.
- Drizzle the chops with the buttermilk and toss into a zipper-type bag with the flour.
- Marinate for 30 mins.
- Arrange the chops in the fryer stacking is okay.
- Spritz using a cooking oil spray.
- Air-fry the chops for 15 mins 380° Fahrenheit.
- Flip after the first 10 mins.
- Serve with your favorite side dishes.

Nutrition Facts: Cal: 147 Protein: 23g Carbs: 6g Fat 3g

8.10 Stuffed Pork Chops

Servings: 3; **Preparation Time**: 15 mins

Cooking Time: 30 mins; **Total Time**: 45 mins

Ingredients:

- 3 Thick-cut pork chops
- 7 Mushrooms
- 1 tbsp. Lemon juice
- 1 tbsp. Almond flour

Directions:

- Heat the Air Fryer to reach 350° Fahrenheit.
- Arrange the pork chops in the Air Fryer.
- Set the timer for 15 mins.
- Chop and sauté the mushrooms for three mins and spritz with lemon juice.
- Toss in the flour and herbs.
- Continue to sauté for four mins and set aside.
- Prepare five sheets of foil for the chops.
- Arrange the chops on the foil and add some of the mushroom fixings.
- Carefully fold the foil to seal in the chop and juices.
- Add the chops in the Air Fryer for 30 mins.

Nutrition Facts: Cal: 90 Protein: 6g Carbs: 2g Fat 6g

8.11 Lamb Ribs - Saltimbocca

Servings: 4; **Preparation Time**: 5 mins

Cooking Time: 15 mins; **Total Time**: 20 mins

Ingredients:

- 2 balls Mozzarella cheese
- 2 lb. Lamb racks
- 4 Thinly sliced pieces of prosciutto
- 4 Sage leaves
- 2 tbsp. Olive oil

Directions:

- Heat the Air Fryer to reach 350° Fahrenheit.
- Slice the racks of lamb into quarters.
- Slice a deep pocket in each of the chops and stuff with thinly sliced cheese pieces.
- Add a sage leaf on top and wrap with sliced prosciutto.
- Spritz using one tablespoon of the oil.
- Set the timer for 15 mins.
- Transfer to a platter and serve.

Nutrition Facts: Cal: 396 Protein: 59.6g Carbs: 1g Fat 15.6g

8.12 Becon Bacon

Servings: 4-6; **Preparation Time**: 10 mins

Cooking Time: 30 mins; **Total Time**: 40 mins

Ingredients:

- 1 lb. Pork tenderloin
- 1-2 tbsp. Dijon mustard
- 3-4 strips Bacon

Directions:

- Set the Air Fryer temperature at 360° Fahrenheit.
- Coat the tenderloin with the mustard and wrap with the bacon.
- Air-fry them for 15 mins.
- Flip and cook 10 to 15 more mins.
- Serve with your favorite sides.

Nutrition Facts: Cal: 340 Protein: 45g Carbs: 1.7g Fat 16.6g

8.13 German Sausage

Servings: 6; **Preparation Time**: 10 mins

Cooking Time: 20 mins; **Total Time**: 30 mins

Ingredients:

- 5 links/1 pkg. Bratwurst Approx.
- 1 each red and green bell pepper
- 1/4 cup Onion - red or purple
- 1/2 tbsp. Gluten-free Cajun seasoning

Directions:

- Warm the unit to reach 390° Fahrenheit.
- Line the Air Fryer with foil, if preferred.
- Slice and add in the vegetables.
- Slice the bratwurst into about 01/2-inch size rounds, and place on top of the veggies.
- Evenly sprinkle the seasoning on top.
- Air-fry for 10 mins. Carefully open and stir or mix.
- Air-fry for another 10 mins before serving.

Nutrition Facts: Cal: 440 Protein: 42g Carbs: 1.7g Fat 16.6g

8.14 English Dumpling

Servings: 2; **Preparation Time**: 5 mins

Cooking Time: 10 mins ; **Total Time**: 15 mins

Ingredients:

- 1/2 lb. Ground pork
- 1 tbsp. Olive oil
- 1/2 tsp. each Black pepper and salt
- half of 1 pkg. Dumpling wrappers

Directions:

- Set the Air Fryer temperature setting at 390° Fahrenheit.
- Mix the fixings together.

- Prepare each dumpling using two teaspoons of the pork mixture.
- Seal the edges with a portion of water to make the triangle form.
- Lightly spritz the Air Fryer basket using a cooking oil spray as needed.
- Add the dumplings to air-fry for eight mins.
- Serve when they're ready.

Nutrition Facts: Cal: 396 Protein: 59.6g Carbs: 1g Fat 15.6g

8.15 Pork Joint

Servings: 10; **Preparation Time**: 10 mins

Cooking Time: 10 mins; **Total Time**: 20 mins

Ingredients:

- 3 cups of Cooked shredded pork tenderloin or chicken
- 10 Flour tortillas, small
- 2 and 1/2 cups Fat-free shredded mozzarella
- 1 Lime juice

Directions:

- Set the Air Fryer at 380° Fahrenheit.
- Sprinkle the juice over the pork.
- Microwave five of the tortillas at a time putting a damp paper towel over them for 10 seconds.
- Add three ounces of pork and ¼ of a cup of cheese to each tortilla.
- Tightly roll the tortillas. Line the tortillas onto a greased foil-lined pan.
- Spray an even coat of cooking oil spray over the tortillas.
- Air Fry for 7 to 10 mins or until the tortillas are a golden color, flipping halfway through.

Nutrition Facts: Cal: 153 Protein: 5.9g Carbs: 5.7g Fat 12g

8.16 Ranch Lamb

Servings: 4; **Preparation Time**: 10 mins

Cooking Time: 10 mins; **Total Time**: 20 mins

Ingredients:

- 4 Center-cut - 1-inch boneless pork chops
- 2 tsp. Dry ranch salad dressing mix - ex. Hidden Valley
- Also Needed: Aluminum foil and cooking oil spray

Directions:

- Warm the Air Fryer to 390° Fahrenheit.
- Lightly spray both sides of the chops and the inside of the Air Fryer basket using a cooking oil spray.
- Sprinkle both sides with the ranch seasoning mix and let it rest at room temperature for ten mins.
- Place the chops in the Air Fryer, working in batches, if necessary, to ensure the fryer isn't overcrowded.
- Cook for five mins.
- Flip the chops and cook five mins more.
- Let it rest on a foil-covered plate for an additional five mins before serving.

Nutrition Facts: Cal: 128 Protein: 9.4g Carbs: 4.8g Fat 14.9g

CHAPTER 9:
Beef Options

9.1 Beef and Potato

Servings: 4; **Preparation Time**: 5 mins

Cooking Time: 10 mins; **Total Time**: 15 mins

Ingredients:

- 3 cups Mashed potatoes
- 1 lb. Ground beef
- 2 Eggs
- 2 tbsp. Garlic powder
- 1 cup Sour cream

Directions:

- Set the Air Fryer to reach 390° Fahrenheit.
- Combine all the fixings in a mixing container.
- Scoop it into a heat-safe dish.
- Arrange in the fryer to cook for two mins.
- Serve for lunch or a quick dinner.

Nutrition Facts: Cal: 396 Protein: 59.6g Carbs: 1g Fat 15.6g

9.2 Beef Roll-Ups

Servings: 4; **Preparation Time**: 10 mins

Cooking Time: 20 mins; **Total Time**: 30 mins

Ingredients:

- 6 slices Provolone cheese
- 2 lbs. Beef flank steak
- 3 tbsp. Pesto
- 3/4 cup Baby spinach
- 3 oz. Roasted red bell peppers

Directions:

- Heat the Air Fryer at 400° Fahrenheit.
- Slice the steak.
- Add the pesto and butter evenly on the meat.

- Layer in the spinach, peppers, and cheese about ¾ of the way down through the roll-up.
- Roll the mixture.
- Secure it with skewers or toothpicks.
- Air-fry for 14 mins.
- Turn the beef halfway through the cooking process.
- Wait for at least ten mins before slicing to serve.

Nutrition Facts: Cal: 450 Protein: 19g Carbs: 10g Fat 40g

9.3 Breaded Beef Schnitzel

Servings: 1; **Preparation Time**: 5 mins

Cooking Time: 15 mins; **Total Time**: 20 mins

Ingredients:

- 2 tbsp. Olive oil
- 1 Thin beef schnitzel
- 1/2 cup Gluten-free breadcrumbs
- 1 Egg

Directions:

- Heat the Air Fryer a couple of mins 356° Fahrenheit.
- Combine the breadcrumbs and oil in a shallow bowl.
- Whisk the egg in another mixing container.
- Dip the beef into the egg, and then the breadcrumbs.
- Arrange in the basket of the Air Fryer.
- Air-fry 12 mins and serve.

Nutrition Facts: Cal: 147 Protein: 23g Carbs: 6g Fat 3g

9.4 Cheeseburger 'Mini' Sliders

Servings: 3; **Preparation Time**: 5 mins

Cooking Time: 10 mins; **Total Time**: 15 mins

Ingredients:

- 6 slices Cheddar cheese
- 1 lb. Ground beef
- Freshly cracked black pepper and salt as desired
- 6 Dinner rolls

Directions:

- Warm the Air Fryer ahead of fry time to 390° Fahrenheit.
- Shape six 21/2-oz. patties and dust with the pepper and salt
- Arrange the burgers in the fryer basket and cook for ten mins.
- Take them out of the cooker and add the cheese.
- Return them to the basket for another minute until the cheese melts.

Nutrition Facts: Cal: 450 Protein: 19g Carbs: 10g Fat 40g

9.5 Quick and Easy Rib Eye Steak

Servings: 1; **Preparation Time**: 5 mins

Cooking Time: 35 mins; **Total Time**: 40 mins

Ingredients:

- 1 about 2 lb. Unchilled steak
- 1 tbsp. Olive oil
- 1 tbsp. Steak Rub
- Salt and pepper mix as desired
- Baking pan also needed to fit into the basket

Directions:

- Press the "M" button for the French Fries icon.

- Adjust the time to four mins at 400° Fahrenheit.
- Rub the steak with the oil and seasonings.
- Arrange the steak in the basket and air-fry for 14 mins.
- Flip it over after seven mins.
- Place the rib eye on a platter, and let it rest for ten mins.
- Slice it and garnish the way you like it.

Nutrition Facts: Cal: 450 Protein: 19g Carbs: 10g Fat 40g

9.6 Roast Beef

Servings: 6; **Preparation Time**: 15 mins

Cooking Time: 55 mins ; **Total Time**:70 mins

Ingredients:

- 1/2 tsp. Garlic powder
- 1/2 tsp. Oregano
- 1 tsp. Dried thyme
- 1 tbsp. Olive oil
- 2 lb. round roast

Directions:

- Heat the Air Fryer at 330° Fahrenheit.
- Combine the spices.
- Brush the oil over the beef and rub it using the spice mixture.
- Add to a baking dish and arrange it in the Air Fryer basket for 30 mins.
- Turn it over and continue cooking 25 more mins.
- Wait for a few mins before slicing.
- Serve on your choice of bread or plain with a delicious side dish.

Nutrition Facts: Cal: 450 Protein: 19g Carbs: 10g Fat 40g

9.7 Sweet and Spicy Montreal Steak

Servings: 2; **Preparation Time**: 5 mins

Cooking Time: 7 mins; **Total Time**: 12 mins

Ingredients:

- 2 Sirloin steaks boneless
- 1 tbsp. Brown sugar
- 1 tbsp. Montreal steak seasoning
- 1 tsp. Crushed red pepper
- 1 tbsp. Olive oil

Directions:

- Set the temperature of the Air Fryer at 390° Fahrenheit.
- Prepare the steaks with oil.
- Rub them with the desired seasonings.
- Arrange the steaks in the basket and set the timer for three mins.
- Flip the steak over and air-fry for another three mins.
- Cool and slice it into strips before serving.

Nutrition Facts: Cal: 260 Protein: 54g Carbs: 45g Fat 65g

9.8 Rose Beef

Servings: 4; **Preparation Time**: 5 mins

Cooking Time: 5 mins; **Total Time**: 10 mins

Ingredients:

- 3 cups Mashed potatoes
- 1 lb. Ground beef
- 2 Eggs
- 2 tbsp. Garlic powder
- 1 cup Sour cream

Directions:

- Set the Air Fryer to reach 390° Fahrenheit.
- Combine all the fixings in a mixing container.
- Scoop it into a heat-safe dish.
- Arrange in the fryer to cook for two mins.
- Serve for lunch or a quick dinner.

Nutrition Facts: Cal: 147 Protein: 23g Carbs: 6g Fat 3g

9.9 Beed Bower

Servings: 4; **Preparation Time**: 10 mins

Cooking Time: 15 mins; **Total Time**: 25 mins

Ingredients:

- 6 slices Provolone cheese
- 2 lbs. Beef flank steak
- 3 tbsp. Pesto
- 3/4 cup Baby spinach
- 3 oz. Roasted red bell peppers

Directions:

- Heat the Air Fryer at 400° Fahrenheit.
- Slice the steak. Add the pesto and butter evenly on the meat.
- Layer in the spinach, peppers, and cheese about ¾ of the way down through the roll-up.
- Roll the mixture.
- Secure it with skewers or toothpicks.
- Air-fry for 14 mins.
- Turn the beef halfway through the cooking process.
- Wait for at least ten mins before slicing to serve.

Nutrition Facts: Cal: 390 Protein: 26g Carbs: 52g Fat 76g

9.10 Beef Schnitzel

Servings: 1; **Preparation Time**: 5 mins

Cooking Time: 12 mins; **Total Time**: 17 mins

Ingredients:

- 2 tbsp. Olive oil
- 1 Thin beef schnitzel
- 1/2 cup Gluten-free breadcrumbs
- 1 Egg

Directions:

- Heat the Air Fryer a couple of mins 356° Fahrenheit.
- Combine the breadcrumbs and oil in a shallow bowl.
- Whisk the egg in another mixing container.
- Dip the beef into the egg, and then the breadcrumbs.
- Arrange in the basket of the Air Fryer.
- Air-fry 12 mins and serve.

Nutrition Facts: Cal: 396 Protein: 59.6g Carbs: 1g Fat 15.6g

9.11 Roast Rosemary

Servings: 6; **Preparation Time**: 5 mins

Cooking Time: 25 mins ; **Total Time**: 30 mins

Ingredients:

- Garlic powder (.5 tsp.)
- Oregano (.5 tsp.)
- Dried thyme (1 tsp.)
- Olive oil (1 tbsp.)
- Round roast (2 lb.)

Directions

- Heat the Air Fryer at 330° Fahrenheit.
- Combine the spices. Brush the oil over the beef, and rub it using the spice mixture.
- Add to a baking dish and arrange it in the

Air Fryer basket for 30 mins. Turn it over and continue cooking 25 more mins.

- Wait for a few mins before slicing.
- Serve on your choice of bread or plain with a delicious side dish.

Nutrition Facts: Cal: 396 Protein: 59.6g Carbs: 1g Fat 15.6g

9.12 Rib Eye Steak

Servings: 1; **Preparation Time**: 5 mins

Cooking Time: 10 mins; **Total Time**: 15 mins

Ingredients:

- Unshelled steak (1 @ about 2 lb.)
- Olive oil (1 tbsp.)
- Steak Rub: Salt and pepper mix (1 tbsp. As desired)
- Baking pan also needed to fit into the basket

Directions

- Press the "M" button for the French Fries icon. Adjust the time to four mins at 400° Fahrenheit.
- Rub the steak with the oil and seasonings. Arrange the steak in the basket and air-fry for 14 mins. (Flip it over after seven mins.)
- Place the rib eye on a platter, and let it rest for ten mins.
- Slice it and garnish the way you like it.

Nutrition Facts: Cal: 396 Protein: 59.6g Carbs: 1g Fat 15.6g

9.13 Burger

Servings: 3; **Preparation Time:** 5 mins

Cooking Time: 10 mins; **Total Time:** 15 mins

Ingredients:

- Cheddar cheese (6 slices)
- Ground beef (1 lb.)
- Freshly cracked black pepper and salt (as desired)
- Dinner rolls (6)

Directions:

- Warm the Air Fryer ahead of fry time to 390° Fahrenheit.
- Shape six (2.5-oz.) patties and dust with the pepper and salt
- Arrange the burgers in the fryer basket and cook for ten mins.
- Take them out of the cooker and add the cheese.
- Return them to the basket for another minute until the cheese melts.

Nutrition Facts: Cal: 396 Protein: 59.6g Carbs: 1g Fat 15.6g

9.14 Sweet Steak

Servings: 2; **Preparation Time:** 5 mins

Cooking Time: 3 mins ; **Total Time:** 8 mins

Ingredients:

- Sirloin steaks 2 boneless
- Brown sugar 1 tbsp.
- Montreal steak seasoning 1 tbsp.
- Crushed red pepper 1 tsp.
- Olive oil 1 tbsp.

Directions

- Set the temperature of the Air Fryer at 390° Fahrenheit.
- Prepare the steaks with oil. Rub them with the desired seasonings.
- Arrange the steaks in the basket and set the timer for three mins.
- Flip the steak over and air-fry for another three mins.
- Cool and slice it into strips before serving.

Nutrition Facts: Cal: 396 Protein: 59.6g Carbs: 1g Fat 15.6g

CHAPTER NO. 10
Seafood Option

10.1 Breaded Coconut Shrimp

Servings: 4; **Preparation Time**: 10 mins

Cooking Time: 15 mins; **Total Time**: 25 mins

Ingredients:

- 1 lb. Shrimp
- 1 cup Panko breadcrumbs
- 1 cup Shredded coconut
- 2 Eggs
- 1/3 cup All-purpose flour

Directions:

- Set the temperature of the Air Fryer at 360° Fahrenheit.
- Peel and devein the shrimp.
- Whisk the seasonings with the flour as desired.
- In another dish, whisk the eggs, and in the third container, combine the breadcrumbs and coconut.
- Dip the cleaned shrimp into the flour, egg wash, and finish it off with the coconut mixture.
- Lightly spray the basket of the fryer and set the timer for 10-15 mins.
- Air-fry until it's a golden brown before serving.

Nutrition Facts: Cal: 450 Protein: 19g Carbs: 10g Fat 40g

10.2 Breaded Cod Sticks

Servings: 5; **Preparation Time**: 5 mins

Cooking Time: 12 mins ; **Total Time**: 17 mins

Ingredients:

- 2 Large eggs
- 3 tbsp. Milk
- 2 cups Breadcrumbs
- 1 cup Almond flour
- 1 lb. Cod

Directions:

- Heat the Air Fryer at 350° Fahrenheit.
- Prepare three bowls: one with the milk and eggs, one with the breadcrumbs salt and pepper if desired, and another with almond flour.
- Dip the sticks in the flour, egg mixture, and breadcrumbs.
- Place in the basket and set the timer for 12 mins.
- Toss the basket halfway through the cooking process.
- Serve with your favorite sauce.

Nutrition Facts: Cal: 450 Protein: 19g Carbs: 10g Fat 40g

10.3 Cajun Salmon

Servings: 1-2; **Preparation Time**: 10 mins

Cooking Time: 12 mins ; **Total Time**: 22 mins

Ingredients:

- 1 - 7 oz. 03/4-inches thick Salmon fillet
- Cajun seasoning
- ¼ of a lemon Juice
- Optional: Sprinkle of sugar

Directions:

- Set the Air Fryer at 356° Fahrenheit to preheat for five mins.
- Rinse and dry the salmon with a paper towel.
- Cover the fish with the Cajun coating mix.
- Place the fillet in the air fryer for seven mins with the skin side up.
- Serve with a sprinkle of lemon and dusting of sugar if desired.

Nutrition Facts: Cal: 243 Protein: 18g Carbs: 2g Fat 17g 0.4

10.4 Cajun Shrimp

Servings: 4-6; **Preparation Time**: 5 mins

Cooking Time: 10 mins; **Total Time**: 15 mins

Ingredients:

- 16-20/11/4 lb. Tiger shrimp
- 1 tbsp. Olive oil
- 1/2 tsp. Old Bay seasoning
- 1/4 tsp. Smoked paprika
- 1/4 tsp. Cayenne pepper

Directions:

- Set the Air Fryer at 390° Fahrenheit.
- Cover the shrimp using the oil and spices.
- Toss them into the Air Fryer basket and set the timer for five mins.
- Serve with your favorite side dish.

Nutrition Facts: Cal: 147 Protein: 23g Carbs: 6g Fat 3g

10.5 Cod Fish Nuggets

Servings: 4; **Preparation Time**: 6 mins

Cooking Time: 20 mins ; **Total Time**: 26 mins

Ingredients:

- 1 lb. Cod fillet
- 3 Eggs
- 4 tbsp. Olive oil
- 1 cup Almond flour
- 1 cup Gluten-free breadcrumbs

Directions:

- Warm the Air Fryer at 390° Fahrenheit.
- Slice the cod into nuggets.
- Prepare three bowls.
- Whisk the eggs in one.
- Combine the salt, oil, and breadcrumbs in another.
- Sift the almond flour into the third one.
- Cover each of the nuggets with the flour, dip in the eggs, and the breadcrumbs.
- Arrange the nuggets in the basket and set the timer for 20 mins.
- Serve the fish with your favorite dips or sides.

Nutrition Facts: Cal: 110 Protein: 9g Carbs: 1g Fat 8g

1

0.6 Creamy Salmon

Servings: 2; **Preparation Time**: 6 mins

Cooking Time: 10 mins ; **Total Time**: 16 mins

Ingredients:

- 1 tbsp. Chopped dill
- 1 tbsp. Olive oil
- 3 tbsp. Sour cream
- 1.76 oz. Plain yogurt
- 6 pieces/3/4 lb. Salmon

Directions:

- Heat the Air Fryer and wait for it to reach 285° Fahrenheit.
- Shake the salt over the salmon and add them to the fryer basket with the olive oil to air-fry for 10 mins.
- Whisk the yogurt, salt, and dill.
- Serve the salmon with the sauce with your favorite sides.

Nutrition Facts: Cal: 353 Protein: 5.9g Carbs: 5.7g Fat 12g

10.7 Crumbled Fish

Servings: 2; **Preparation Time**: 7 mins

Cooking Time: 12 mins ; **Total Time**: 19 mins

Ingredients:

- 1/2 cup Breadcrumbs
- 4 tbsp. Vegetable oil
- 1 Egg
- 4 Fish fillets
- 1 Lemon

Directions:

- Heat the Air Fryer to reach 356° Fahrenheit.
- Whisk the oil and breadcrumbs until crumbly.
- Dip the fish into the egg, then the crumb mixture.

- Arrange the fish in the cooker and air-fry for 12 mins.
- Garnish using the lemon.

Nutrition Facts: Cal: 328 Protein: 9.4g Carbs: 4.8g Fat 14.9g

10. 8Easy Crab Sticks

Servings: 2-3; **Preparation Time**: 5 mins

Cooking Time: 10 mins ; **Total Time**: 15 mins

Ingredients:

- 1 package Crab sticks
- Cooking oil spray as needed

Directions:

- Take each of the sticks out of the package and unroll it until the stick is flat.
- Tear the sheets into thirds.
- Arrange them on a baking tray and lightly spritz using cooking spray.
- Set the timer for 10 mins.
- Note: If you shred the crab meat, you can cut the time in half, but they will also easily fall through the holes in the basket.

Nutrition Facts: Cal: 340 Protein: 45g Carbs: 1.7g Fat 16.6g

10.9 Fried Catfish

Servings: 3; **Preparation Time**: 5 mins

Cooking Time: 13 mins ; **Total Time**: 18 mins

Ingredients:

- 1 tbsp. Olive oil
- 1/4 cup Seasoned fish fry
- 4 Catfish fillets

Directions:

- Heat the Air Fryer to reach 400° Fahrenheit before fry time.
- Rinse the catfish and pat dry using a paper

towel.

- Dump the seasoning into a sizeable zipper-type bag.
- Add the fish and shake to cover each fillet.
- Spray with a spritz of cooking oil spray and add to the basket.
- Set the timer for 10 mins.
- Flip, and reset the timer for ten additional mins.
- Turn the fish once more and cook for 2-3 mins.
- Once it reaches the desired crispiness, transfer to a plate, and serve.

Nutrition Facts: Cal: 153 Protein: 5.9g Carbs: 5.7g Fat 12g

10.10 Simple Shrimp

Servings: 4; **Preparation Time**: 5 mins

Cooking Time: 15 mins; **Total Time**: 20 mins

Ingredients:

- 1 lb. Shrimp
- 1 cup Panko breadcrumbs
- 1 cup Shredded coconut
- 2 Eggs
- 1/3 cup All-purpose flour

Directions:

- Set the temperature of the Air Fryer at 360° Fahrenheit.
- Peel and devein the shrimp.
- Whisk the seasonings with the flour as desired.
- In another dish, whisk the eggs, and in the third container, combine the breadcrumbs and coconut.
- Dip the cleaned shrimp into the flour, egg wash, and finish it off with the coconut mixture.
- Lightly spray the basket of the fryer and

set the timer for 10-15 mins.

- Air-fry until it's a golden brown before serving.

Nutrition Facts: Cal: 353 Protein: 5.9g Carbs: 5.7g Fat 12g

10.11 Cajun Shrimp

Servings: 4-6; **Preparation Time**: 5 mins

Cooking Time: 5 mins; **Total Time**: 10 mins

Ingredients:

- Tiger shrimp (16-20/1.25 lb.)
- Olive oil (1 tbsp.)
- Old Bay seasoning (.5 tsp.)
- Smoked paprika (.25 tsp.)
- Cayenne pepper (.25 tsp.)

Directions:

- Set the Air Fryer at 390° Fahrenheit.
- Cover the shrimp using the oil and spices.
- Toss them into the Air Fryer basket and set the timer for five mins.
- Serve with your favorite side dish.

Nutrition Facts: Cal: 243 Protein: 18g Carbs: 2g Fat 17g

10.12 Fish fingers

Servings: 4; **Preparation Time**: 10 mins

Cooking Time: 10 mins; **Total Time**: 20 mins

Ingredients:

- Cod fillet (1 lb.)
- Eggs (3)
- Olive oil (4 tbsp.)
- Almond flour (1 cup)
- Gluten-free breadcrumbs (1 cup)

Directions:

- Warm the Air Fryer at 390° Fahrenheit.
- Slice the cod into nuggets.

- Prepare three bowls. Whisk the eggs in one. Combine the salt, oil, and breadcrumbs in another. Sift the almond flour into the third one.
- Cover each of the nuggets with the flour, dip in the eggs, and the breadcrumbs.
- Arrange the nuggets in the basket and set the timer for 20 mins.
- Serve the fish with your favorite dips or sides.

Nutritional Facts: Cal: 300 Fat: 22 g Carbs: 89 g Protein: 100 g

10.13 Catfish

Servings: 3; **Preparation Time**: 5 mins

Cooking Time: 14 mins; **Total Time**: 19 mins

Ingredients:

- Olive oil (1 tbsp.)
- Seasoned fish fry (.25 cup)
- Catfish fillets (4)

Directions:

- Heat the Air Fryer to reach 400° Fahrenheit before fry time.
- Rinse the catfish and pat dry using a paper towel.
- Dump the seasoning into a sizeable zipper-type bag. Add the fish and shake to cover each fillet. Spray with a spritz of cooking oil spray and add to the basket.
- Set the timer for 10 mins. Flip, and reset the timer for ten additional mins. Turn the fish once more and cook for 2-3 mins.
- Once it reaches the desired crispiness, transfer to a plate, and serve.

Nutrition Facts: Cal: 340 Protein: 45g Carbs: 1.7g Fat 16.6g

10.14 Fish Cake

Servings: 2; **Preparation Time**: 3 mins

Cooking Time: 10 mins; **Total Time**: 13 mins

Ingredients:

- Chopped dill (1 tbsp.)
- Olive oil (1 tbsp.)
- Sour cream (3 tbsp.)
- Plain yogurt (1.76 oz.)
- Salmon (6 pieces)/.75 lb.)

Directions:

- Heat the Air Fryer and wait for it to reach 285° Fahrenheit.
- Shake the salt over the salmon and add them to the fryer basket with the olive oil to air-fry for 10 mins.
- Whisk the yogurt, salt, and dill.
- Serve the salmon with the sauce with your favorite sides.

Nutrition Facts: Cal: 147 Protein: 23g Carbs: 6g Fat 3g

10.15 Salmon

Servings: 1-2; **Preparation Time**: 5 mins

Cooking Time: 7 mins; **Total Time**: 12 mins

Ingredients:

- Salmon fillet (1 - 7 oz.) 0.75-inches thick
- Cajun seasoning
- Juice (¼ of a lemon)
- Optional: Sprinkle of sugar

Directions:

- Set the Air Fryer at 356° Fahrenheit to preheat for five mins.
- Rinse and dry the salmon with a paper

towel. Cover the fish with the Cajun coating mix.

- Place the fillet in the air fryer for seven mins with the skin side up.
- Serve with a sprinkle of lemon and dusting of sugar if desired.

Nutrition Facts: Cal: 340 Protein: 45g Carbs: 1.7g Fat 16.6g

10.16 Caspian Cod

Servings: 5; **Preparation Time**: 5 mins

Cooking Time: 10 mins; **Total Time**: 15 mins

Ingredients:

- Large eggs (2)
- Milk (3 tbsp.)
- Breadcrumbs (2 cups)
- Almond flour (1 cup)
- Cod (1 lb.)

Directions:

- Heat the Air Fryer at 350° Fahrenheit.
- Prepare three bowls; one with the milk and eggs, one with the breadcrumbs (salt and pepper if desired), and another with almond flour.
- Dip the sticks in the flour, egg mixture, and breadcrumbs.
- Place in the basket and set the timer for 12 mins. Toss the basket halfway through the cooking process.
- Serve with your favorite sauce.

Nutritional Facts: Cal: 300 Fat: 22 g Carbs: 89 g Protein: 100 g

10.17 Sticks

Servings: 2-3; **Preparation Time**: 5 mins

Cooking Time: 5 mins; **Total Time**: 10 mins

Ingredients:

- Crab sticks (1 package)
- Cooking oil spray (as needed)

Directions:

- Take each of the sticks out of the package and unroll it until the stick is flat. Tear the sheets into thirds.
- Arrange them on a baking tray and lightly spritz using cooking spray. Set the timer for 10 mins.

Note: If you shred the crab meat, you can cut the time in half, but they will also easily fall through the holes in the basket.

Nutrition Facts: Cal: 243 Protein: 18g Carbs: 2g Fat 17g

10.18 Fish Taste

Servings: 2; **Preparation Time**: 2 mins

Cooking Time: 12 mins ; **Total Time**: 14 mins

Ingredients:

- Breadcrumbs (.5 cup)
- Vegetable oil (4 tbsp.)
- Egg (1)
- Fish fillets (4)
- Lemon (1)

Directions:

- Heat the Air Fryer to reach 356° Fahrenheit.
- Whisk the oil and breadcrumbs until crumbly.
- Dip the fish into the egg, then the crumb mixture.
- Arrange the fish in the cooker and air-fry for 12 mins.
- Garnish using the lemon.

Nutrition Facts: Cal: 541 Protein: 16g Carbs: 2g Fat 61g

CHAPTER 11:
Desserts

11.1 Air-Fried Plantains

Servings: 4; **Preparation Time**: 5 mins

Cooking Time: 13 mins ; **Total Time**: 18 mins

Ingredients:

- 2 tsp. Avocado or sunflower oil
- 2 Ripened/almost brown – plantains
- 1/8 tsp. Optional: Salt

Directions:

- Warm up the Air Fryer to 400° Fahrenheit.
- Slice the plantains at an angle for a 1/2-inch thickness.
- Mix the oil, salt, and plantains in a container – making sure you coat the surface thoroughly.
- Set the timer for eight to ten mins; shake after five mins.
- If they are not done to your liking, add a minute or two more.

Nutrition Facts: Cal: 340 Protein: 45g Carbs: 1.7g Fat 16.6g

11.2 Air-Fried S'mores

Servings: 4; **Preparation Time**: 5 mins

Cooking Time: 6 mins ; **Total Time**: 11 mins

Ingredients:

- 4 Whole graham crackers
- 2 Marshmallows
- 4 pieces Chocolate - such as Hershey's

Directions:

- Break the graham crackers in half to make eight squares.
- Cut the marshmallows in half crosswise with a pair of scissors.
- Place the marshmallows cut lateral down on four graham squares.
- Put marshmallow up in the basket of the Air Fryer and heat on 390° Fahrenheit for four to five mins, or until golden.
- Remove them from the fryer and place a piece Break all graham crackers in half to create eight squares.
- Cut marshmallows in half crosswise with a pair of scissors.
- Place the marshmallows, cut side down, on four graham squares of chocolate and graham square on top of each toasted marshmallow and serve.

Nutrition Facts: Cal: 243 Protein: 18g Carbs: 2g Fat 17g

11.3 Apple Chips

Servings: 2; **Preparation Time**: 5 mins

Cooking Time: 8 mins ; **Total Time**: 13 mins

Ingredients:

- 1/2 tsp. Cinnamon
- 1 Apple
- 1 tbsp. Sugar
- 1 pinch kosher salt

Directions:

- Warm the Air Fryer in advance to reach 390° Fahrenheit.
- Slice the apples lengthwise and arrange them in a dish with the cinnamon, sugar, and salt.
- Toss.

- Cook them until they are crispy or around seven to eight mins.
- Turn halfway through the cycle.
- Transfer to a platter and serve.

Nutrition Facts: Cal: 153 Protein: 5.9g Carbs: 5.7g Fat 12g

11.4 Banana S'mores

Servings: 4; **Preparation Time**: 6 mins

Cooking Time: 8 mins ; **Total Time**: 14 mins

Ingredients:

- 4 Bananas
- 3 tbsp. Mini-peanut butter chips
- 3 tbsp. Graham cracker cereal
- 3 tbsp. Mini-chocolate chips - semi-sweet

Directions:

- Heat the Air Fryer in advance at 400° Fahrenheit.
- Slice the bananas lengthwise with the inside of the curve.
- Don't slice through the lowest of the peel.
- Open slightly - forming a pocket.
- Fill each pocket with chocolate chips, peanut butter chips, and marshmallows.
- Poke the cereal into the filling.
- Arrange the stuffed bananas in the fryer basket, keeping them upright with the filling facing up.
- Air-fry until the peel has blackened, and the chocolate and marshmallows have toasted 6 mins.
- Chill for 1-2 mins.
- Spoon out the filling to serve.

Nutrition Facts: Cal: 128 Protein: 9.4g Carbs: 4.8g Fat 14.9g

11.5 Cherry Pie

Servings: 8; **Preparation Time**: 6 mins

Cooking Time: 15 mins; **Total Time**: 21 mins

Ingredients:

- 21 oz. Cherry pie filling can
- 1 tbsp. Milk
- 2 Refrigerated pie crusts
- 1 Egg yolk

Directions:

- Warm the fryer at 310° Fahrenheit.
- Poke holes into the crust after placing it in a pie plate.
- Allow the excess to hang over the edges.
- Place in the Air Fryer for five 5 mins.
- Transfer the basket with the pie plate onto the countertop.
- Fill it with the cherries.
- Remove the excess crust.
- Cut the remaining crust into ¾-inch strips - weaving a lattice across the pie.
- Make an egg wash using the milk and egg.
- Brush the pie. Air-fry for 15 mins.
- Serve with a scoop of ice cream.

Nutrition Facts: Cal: 147 Protein: 23g Carbs: 6g Fat 3g

11.6 Easy Bacon

Servings: 8; **Preparation Time**: 5 mins

Cooking Time: 12 mins ; **Total Time**: 17 mins

Ingredients:

- 12 oz. Bacon

Directions:

- Set the Air Fryer temperature at 350° Fahrenheit for ten mins.
- Arrange the bacon in a single layer in the Air Fryer.
- Set the timer for 10 mins.
- Check for the desired crispiness and air-fry for an additional one to two mins.

- Between the batches, drain the grease. Serve as desired.

Nutrition Facts: Cal: 250 Protein: 19g Carbs: 10g Fat 40g

11.7 Fluffy Peanut Butter Marshmallow Turnovers

Servings: 4;: **Preparation Time**: 5 mins

Cooking Time: 10 mins; **Total Time**: 15 mins

Ingredients:

- 4 defrosted sheets Filo pastry
- 4 tbsp. Chunky peanut butter
- 2 oz. Melted butter
- 4 tsp. Marshmallow fluff
- 1 pinch Sea salt

Directions:

- Set the temperature of the Air Fryer at 360° Fahrenheit.
- Use the melted butter to brush one sheet of the filo.
- Put the second sheet on top and brush it also with butter.
- Continue the process until you have completed all four sheets.
- Cut the layers into four—12-inch x 3-inch strips.
- Place one teaspoon of the marshmallow fluff on the underside and one tablespoon of the peanut butter.
- Fold the tip over the filo strip to form a triangle, making sure the filling is completely wrapped.
- Seal the ends with a small amount of butter.
- Place the completed turnovers into the Air Fryer for three to five mins.
- When done, they will be fluffy and golden brown.

- Add a touch of sea salt for the sweet/salty combo.
- Notes: The Filo/Phyllo pastry is a little different than regular pastry.
- It is tissue-thin and has very little fat content.
- It is considered okay by some bakers and is interchange the filo with regular puff pastry for turnovers.

Nutrition Facts: Cal: 310 Protein: 9g Carbs: 1g Fat 8g

11.8 Funnel Cake Bites

Servings: 8; **Preparation Time**: 6 mins

Cooking Time: 12 mins ; **Total Time**: 18 mins

Ingredients:

- 1 cup Greek yogurt
- 1 cup - divided Self-rising flour
- For Dusting: Powdered sugar
- Optional: 1 tbsp. Vanilla bean paste

Directions:

- Heat the Air Fryer at 375° Fahrenheit.
- Combine the yogurt, ¾ of the flour, and vanilla if using.
- Roll out the dough using the remainder of the flour.
- Slice it into 32 squares and place in the Air Fryer 8 at a time.
- Set the timer for 4 mins.
- Flip then over and continue to air-fry for another 3 to 4 mins until ready.
- Lightly dust with the sugar as desired and serve.

Nutrition Facts: Cal: 128 Protein: 9.4g Carbs: 4.8g Fat 14.9g

11.9 Healthy Pop-Tarts

Servings: 6; **Preparation Time**: 25 mins

Cooking Time: 30 mins; **Total Time**: 55 mins

Ingredients:

- 1/3 cup or 8 oz. - quartered Strawberries
- 1/4 cup Granulated sugar
- 14.1 oz. pkg. Use 1 Refrigerated pie crusts
- 2 oz. Powdered sugar
- 2 tsp. lemon juice

Directions:

- In a microwave-safe bowl of medium size, mix together the chopped strawberries and granulated sugar.
- After 15 mins, whisk the ingredients periodically while allowing them to sit and rest.
- Microwave on high for about ten mins, stirring once halfway through cooking, until the liquid is reduced and glossy.
- Allow to totally cool for approximately half an hour.
- On a surface dusted with flour, roll out the pie crust into a circle measuring 12 inches in diameter. Rerolling any scraps of dough as necessary, divide the dough into 12 rectangles measuring 2 1/2 inches by 3 inches.
- Place about two tablespoons worth of the strawberry mixture in the middle of six of the dough rectangles, leaving a border of half an inch all the way around.
- Apply a thin layer of water around the edges of the filled dough rectangles, then top with the remaining dough rectangles and press the edges with a fork to seal.
- Use a cooking oil spray to thoroughly coat the tarts.
- Arrange three tarts in a single layer into the basket of the Air Fryer. Cook at 350 degrees Fahrenheit for ten mins, or until the crust is golden brown, whichever comes first.
- Continue in this manner with the remaining tarts. After about half an hour, transfer to a wire rack to finish cooling fully.
- In a small bowl, combine the powdered sugar and the lemon juice, and whisk together until smooth.
- Once the tarts have cooled, drizzle the glaze over them.
- If you'd like, you can top it off with some sugar sprinkles.

Nutrition Facts: Cal: 390 Protein: 26g Carbs: 52g Fat 76g

11.10 Molten Lava Cakes

Servings: 4; **Preparation Time**: 25 mins

Cooking Time: 30 mins; **Total Time**: 55 mins

Ingredients:

- 2 Eggs
- 31/2 oz. Unsalted butter
- 31/2 tbsp. Baker's Sugar - not powdered
- 11/2 tbsp. Self-rising flour
- 31/2 oz. Dark chocolate - chopped pieces
- Also Needed: 4 Standard-sized oven-safe ramekins and microwave- safe bowl

Directions:

- Warm the Air Fryer to 375° Fahrenheit.
- Grease and flour the ramekins.
- Melt the butter and chocolate in the microwave for 3 mins using "7" 3 min.
- Stirring thoroughly.
- Whisk the sugar and eggs until the mixture is pale and frothy.
- Mix the chocolate mixture with the egg mixture.

- Sift and mix in the flour.
- Fill the ramekins about ¾ of the way to full of the cake.
- Set the timer for 10 mins.
- Remove them from the fryer and cool in ramekins for two mins.
- Flip the ramekins upside down onto a plate, tapping the bottom to loosen edges.
- The center should appear dark/gooey.
- Serve warm with a raspberry drizzle.

Nutrition Facts: Cal: 450 Protein: 19g Carbs: 10g Fat 40g

11.11 Plain Cheesecake

Servings: 15; **Preparation Time**: 5 mins

Cooking Time: 15 mins; **Total Time**: 20 mins

Ingredients:

- Unsalted butter (2 tbsp.)
- Honey graham cracker crumbs (1 cup)
- Cream cheese (1 lb.)
- Large eggs (2)
- Vanilla extract (Half tsp.)

Directions:

- Set the Air Fryer to reach 350° Fahrenheit.
- Cut a hole in the center of a piece of parchment paper and place it into the baking dish.
- Combine the graham cracker crust and the butter. Press the mixture into the baking pan. Air-fry for four mins
- Blend the sugar and cream cheese with a mixer, adding one egg at a time until the mixture is creamy. Pour in the vanilla and stir well.
- Pour the cheese mixture into the top of the crust and place it back into the Air Fryer for 15 mins lowering the heat to 310° Fahrenheit.

- Place in the fridge for about three hours before serving.

Nutrition Facts: Cal: 396 Protein: 59.6g Carbs: 1g Fat 15.6g

11.12 Yogurt Pineapple Sticks

Servings: 4; **Preparation Time**: 5 mins

Cooking Time: 10 mins; **Total Time**: 15 mins

Ingredients:

- Pineapple (half of 1)
- Desiccated coconut (.25 cup)

The Dip:

- Fresh mint (1 small sprig)
- Vanilla yogurt (1 cup)

Directions:

- Warm the Air Fryer to reach 392° Fahrenheit.
- Slice the pineapple into stick segments. Dip the chunks of pineapple into the coconut. Arrange the sticks of pineapple into the cooker basket and air-fry for ten mins.
- Dice the mint into fine pieces and mix in with the yogurt.
- Empty the dip into a serving dish. Arrange the baked sticks around the dip to serve.

Nutrition Facts: Cal: 396 Protein: 59.6g Carbs: 1g Fat 15.6g

11.13 Delicious Brownies

Preparation Time: 10 minutes

Cooking Time: 33 minutes

Total Time: 43 minutes

Servings: 6

Ingredients:

- 2 eggs
- ½ cup walnuts, chopped
- ¼ cup all-purpose flour
- 1 cup brown sugar
- 1 ½ tsp vanilla
- ¼ cup of cocoa powder
- ½ cup butter
- Pinch of salt

Directions:

- Spray air fryer shallow baking dish with cooking spray and set aside.
- In a microwave-safe bowl, combine together butter and cocoa powder and microwave until butter is melted. Stir to combine and set aside to cool.
- Once the butter mixture is cool then whisk in eggs and vanilla.
- Stir in brown sugar, walnuts, flour, and salt.
- Pour the batter into the prepared baking dish and bake in instant vortex Air Fryer at 320 F for 33 minutes
- Allow to cool completely then slice and serve.

Nutrition: Calories 343 Fat 23.5 g Carbs 30.9 g Protein 5.7 g

11.14 Blueberry Scones

Preparation Time: 10 minutes

Cooking Time: 10 Minutes

Total Time: 20 minutes

Servings: 10

Ingredients:

- 1 cup white flour
- 1 cup blueberries
- 2 eggs
- ½ cup heavy cream
- ½ cup butter
- 5 tbsp sugar
- 2 tbsp vanilla extract
- 2 tbsp baking powder

Directions:

- Mix in flour, baking powder, salt and blueberries in a bowl and turn.
- Mix heavy cream with vanilla extract, sugar, butter and eggs and turn properly.
- Blend the 2 mixtures, squeeze till dough is ready, obtain 10 triangles from mix, put on baking sheet into air fryer and cook them at 320°F for 10 minutes
- Serve cold.

Nutrition: Calories 525 Fat 21g Carbs 37g Protein 6

11.15 Lemon Cream

Preparation Time: 10 minutes

Cooking Time: 25 minutes

Total Time: 35 minutes

Servings: 4

Ingredients:

- 2 eggs, whisked
- 3 tablespoons sugar
- 2 cups heavy cream
- Juice and zest of 1 lemon
- 2 tablespoons butter, melted
- 1 teaspoon vanilla extract
- ½ teaspoon lemon extract
- Cooking spray

Directions:

- In a bowl, combine the eggs with the sugar and the other ingredients except the cooking spray and stir well.
- Grease a ramekin that fits the air fryer with the cooking spray, pour the mixture inside, put the pan in the air fryer and cook at 360 degrees F for 25 minutes
- Divide into bowls and serve.

Nutrition: Calories 212, Fat 15, Carbs 6 Protein 4

11.16 Mango Cupcakes

Preparation Time: 5 minutes

Cooking Time: 20 minutes

Total Time: 25 minutes

Servings: 4

Ingredients:

- ½ cup almond flour
- ½ cup cocoa powder
- 4 tablespoons sugar
- ½ cup mango, peeled and cubed
- 1 teaspoon baking powder
- 4 eggs, whisked
- 1 teaspoon almond extract
- 4 tablespoons avocado oil
- ¼ cup almond milk
- Cooking spray

Directions:

- In a bowl, mix the flour with the cocoa powder and the other ingredients except the cooking spray and whisk well.
- Grease a cupcake tin that fits the air fryer with the cooking spray, pour the mix inside, put the pan in your air fryer, cook at 350 degrees F for 20 minutes and serve cold.

Nutrition: Calories 103 Fat 4, Carbs 6 Protein 3

11.17 Almond Cookies

Preparation Time: 10 minutes

Cooking Time: 20 minutes

Total Time: 30 minutes

Servings: 8

Ingredients:

- 2 eggs, whisked
- 1 tablespoon coconut cream
- ½ cup almonds, chopped
- 3 tablespoons sugar
- ½ cup butter, melted
- 1 teaspoon vanilla extract
- 2 cups coconut flour
- Cooking spray

Directions:

- In a bowl, mix the eggs with the almonds, cream and the other ingredients except the cooking spray and stir well.
- Shape 8 balls out of this mix, put them on a baking sheet that fits the air fryer greased with cooking spray and flatten them.
- Put the baking sheet in the air fryer, cook at 370 degrees F for 20 minutes and serve the cookies cold.

Nutrition: Calories 234 Fat 13 Carbs 4 Protein 7

11.18 Peanut Butter Cookies

Preparation Time: 10 minutes

Cooking Time: 5 minutes

Total Time: 15 minutes

Servings: 24

Ingredients:

- 1 egg lightly beaten
- 1 cup of sugar
- 1 cup creamy peanut butter

Directions:

- In a mixing bowl, mix together egg sugar, and peanut butter until well combined.
- Spray Air Fryer tray with cooking spray.
- Using ice cream scooper scoop out cookie onto the tray and flattened them using a fork.
- Bake cookie at 350 F for 5 minutes
- Cook remaining cookie batches using the same temperature.
- Serve and enjoy.

Nutrition: Calories 97 Fat 5.6 g Carbs 10.5 g Protein 2.9 g

11.19 Blueberry Lemon Muffins

Preparation Time: 5 Minutes

Cooking Time: 10 Minutes

Total Time: 15 minutes

Servings: 12

Ingredients:

- 1 tsp. vanilla
- Juice and zest of 1 lemon
- Eggs
- 1 C. blueberries
- ½ C. cream
- ¼ C. avocado oil
- ½ C. monk fruit
- ½ C. almond flour

Directions:

- Mix monk fruit and flour together.
- In another bowl, mix vanilla, egg lemon juice, and cream together. Add mixtures together and blend well.
- Spoon batter into cupcake holders
- Place in the Air Fryer. Bake 10 minutes at 320 degrees, checking at 6 minutes to ensure you don't over bake them.

Nutrition: Calories 317 Fat11g Protein3g Carbs: 5g

11.20 Healthy Oatmeal Cookies

Preparation Time: 10 minutes

Cooking Time: 5 minutes

Total Time: 15 minutes

Servings: 8

Ingredients:

- 1 egg lightly beaten
- ¾ cup dried cranberries
- 2 cups old fashioned oats
- 1 tsp vanilla
- 1 stick butter
- 1 ½ cups brown sugar
- ½ tsp baking soda
- ½ tsp ground nutmeg
- 1 tsp cinnamon
- ½ cup can pumpkin
- 1 cup flour
- Pinch of salt

Directions:

- Add all ingredients into the mixing bowl and mix until well combined.
- Spray Air Fryer pan with cooking spray.
- Using scooper scoop cookie dough onto the prepared pan and bake at 350 F for 5 minutes
- Serve and enjoy.

Nutrition: Calories 318 Fat 12.9 g Carbs 47.2 g Protein 4.1 g

11.21 Chocolaty Banana Muffins

Preparation Time: 5 Minutes
Cooking Time: 25 Minutes
Total Time: 30 minutes **Servings:** 12
Ingredients:

- ¾ cup whole wheat flour
- ¾ cup plain flour
- ¼ cup cocoa powder
- ¼ teaspoon baking powder
- 1 teaspoon baking soda
- ¼ teaspoon salt
- Large bananas, peeled and mashed
- 1 cup sugar
- 1/3 cup canola oil
- 1 egg
- ½ teaspoon vanilla essence
- 1 cup mini chocolate chips

Directions:

- In a large bowl, mix together flour, cocoa powder, baking powder, baking soda, and salt.
- In another bowl, add bananas, sugar, oil, egg and vanilla extract and beat till well combined.
- Slowly, add flour mixture in egg mixture and mix till just combined.
- Fold in chocolate chips.
- Preheat the Air Fryer to 345 degrees F. Grease 12 muffin molds.
- Transfer the mixture into prepared muffin molds evenly and Cook it for about 20-25 minutes or till a toothpick inserted in the center comes out clean.
- Remove the muffin molds from Air Fryer and keep on wire rack to cool for about 10 minutes carefully turn on a wire rack to cool completely before serving.

Nutrition: Calories 236 Fat 13g Protein 12g Carbs: 7.7g

11.22 Cinnamon Toast

Preparation Time: 10 Minutes

Cooking Time: 5 Minutes

Total Time: 15 minutes

Servings: 6

Ingredients:

- 2 tsp. pepper
- 1 ½ tsp. vanilla extract
- 1 ½ tsp. cinnamon
- ½ C. sweetener of choice
- 1 C. coconut oil
- 12 slices whole wheat bread

Directions:

- Melt coconut oil and mix with sweetener until dissolved. Mix in remaining ingredients minus bread till incorporated.
- Spread mixture onto bread, covering all area.
- Pour the coated pieces of bread into the Oven rack/basket. Place the Rack on the middle-shelf of the Air Fryer. Set temperature to 400°F, and set time to 5 minutes
- Remove and cut diagonally. Enjoy!

Nutrition: Calories 124; Fat 2g Protein 0g Carbs: 4g

CHAPTER NO. 12 2
2-Week Bonus Meal Plan

12.1 Week 1

Monday

Easy Sausage Patties

Chicken & Salsa

Lemon Spinach Rigatoni

Tuesday

Keto Oatmeal

Sweet Steak with easy bacon

Chicken & Salsa

Wednesday

Egg Cups to Go

English Dumpling

Rose Beef with cherry pie

Thursday

Egg Cups to Go

Chicken & Salsa with Lemon Spinach Rigatoni

Chickpea and Brown Rice Bake

Friday

Keto Oatmeal

Green Peas and Cauliflower Bake

Lemon Spinach Rigatoni

Saturday

English Dumpling

Chickpea and Brown Rice Bake

Rose Beef

Sunday

12.2 Week 2

Monday

Keto Oatmeal

English Dumpling

Crepe Chicken

Tuesday

Eggs and marinara

Pork Joints

Cardamom-Orange Carrots with Chives

Wednesday

Betty's Pancakes with scrambled eggs

Easy Sausage Patties and lemon ice cream

Thursday

Mediterranean Omelet

Scallion Tofu

Crepe Chicken with cherry pie

Friday

Coconut Pancakes

Cheesy Chicken with molten lava cakes

Crepe Chicken and funnel cake bites

Saturday

Scrambled eggs with air fried Bagels

Easy Sausage Patties with chicken bits

Hawaiian Pizzas with banana s'mores

Sunday

Coconut Pancakes

Cardamom-Orange Carrots with Chives

Becon Bacon with healthy pop tarts

CONCLUSION

In the end, it's a cool technology to have in your possession. It can satisfy your cravings to consume all of the mouthwatering and tasty fried food, but without any oil. The results are superior to those achieved by frying in oil and keeping your kitchen clean. Although it performs a respectable job of cooking different types of meat and veggies, the air fryer truly excels in simulating the experience of deep frying. If you like frying meals but don't want to take in as much oil and fat as you normally would, investing in an air fryer is a good idea since it has several perks that make it a worthy investment. Air fryers can often reach the desired temperatures faster than deep fryers can, and they also allow greater control over the level of crispiness achieved with the meal. It is helpful to have some familiarity with the operation of traditional ovens and deep-fat fryers to comprehend how air fryers function. Most traditional ovens get their heat from an open fire or electric heating elements. This heat is then transferred to the air within the oven chamber, where it cooks whatever food is put inside. The air is solely employed in this system to transport energy from the source, which might be an electrical heating coil or open flame, into whatever can transmit that energy into the food being cooked - often by convection, air, or conduction. People who are interested in leading a healthier lifestyle while also reducing the time spent in the kitchen would benefit greatly from using an air fryer. They remove the guesswork from cooking since all you have to do to alter the temperature is turn the dial higher or lower, depending on the dish you are preparing. Therefore, air fryers will become your new best buddy if you're looking to cook French fries, onion rings, chicken wings, or any other food that demands frying at a high temperature.

Made in the USA
Monee, IL
01 June 2023